Tom Taylor

Mary Warner

A Domestic Drama in Four Acts

Tom Taylor

Mary Warner
A Domestic Drama in Four Acts

ISBN/EAN: 9783744670401

Printed in Europe, USA, Canada, Australia, Japan

Cover: Foto ©Thomas Meinert / pixelio.de

More available books at **www.hansebooks.com**

A COMEDY IN THREE ACTS.

BY

Charles Townsend.

PRICE 25 Cents.

This latest play by Mr. Townsend will probably be one of his most popular productions; it certainly is one of his best. It is full of action from start to finish. Comic situations follow one after another, and the act-endings are especially strong and and lively. Every character is good and affords abundant opportunity for effective work. Can be played by four men and three women if desired. The same scene is used for all the acts, and it is an easy interior. A most excellent play for repertoire companies. No seeker for a good play can afford to ignore it.

CHARACTERS.

CAPT. ROBERT RACKET, one of the National Guard. A lawyer when he has nothing else to do, and a liar all the time...........
Comedy Lead

OBADIAH DAWSON, his uncle, from Japan "where they make tea"..*Comedy Old Man*.

TIMOTHY TOLMAN, his friend, who married for money and is sorry for it ....*Juvenile Man*.

MR. DALROY, his father in-law, a jolly old cove.......*Eccentric*.

HOBSON, a waiter from the "Cafe Gloriana," who adds to the confusion..*Utility*.

CLARICE, the Captain's pretty wife, out for a lark, and up to "anything awful"................................*Comedy Lead*.

MRS. TOLMAN, a lady with a temper, who finds her Timothy a vexation of spirit................................*Old Woman*

KATY, a mischievous maid........................*Soubrette*.

TOOTSY, the "Kid," Tim's olive branch.................*Prop*

SYNOPSIS.

ACT. I. Place: Tim's country home on the Hudson near New York. Tim.. A breezy morning in September. The Captain's fancy takes a flight and trouble begins.

ACT. II. Place; the same: Time; the next morning. How one yarn requires another. "The greatest liar unhung," Now the trouble increases and the Captain prepares for war.

ACT. III. Place: the same. Time: evening of the same day. More misery. A general muddle. "Dance or you'll die." Cornered at last. The Captain owns up. All serene.

Time of playing: Two hours.

*Order a sample copy, and see for yourself what a
good play it is.*

A Domestic Drama,

IN FOUR ACTS.

By TOM TAYLOR,

Author of " *Ticket-of-Leave-Man*," " *Henry Dunbar*," " *The Serf*," " *Plot and Passion*," *etc., etc.*

AS FIRST PERFORMED AT THE HAYMARKET THEATRE, LONDON,
UNDER THE MANAGEMENT OF MR. J. B. BUCKSTONE,
ON MONDAY, JUNE 21, 1869.

TO WHICH IS ADDED

A DESCRIPTION OF THE COSTUMES—CAST OF THE CHARACTERS—EN-
TRANCES AND EXITS—RELATIVE POSITIONS OF THE PER-
FORMERS ON THE STAGE, AND THE WHOLE
OF THE STAGE BUSINESS.

————

CHICAGO:

THE DRAMATIC PUBLISHING COMPANY.

CAST OF CHARACTERS.

Haymarket Theatre,
London, June 1st, 1869.

George Warner, a young Engineer, (Tragedy Lead).............Mr. Howe.
Bob Levitt, one of his Fellow-Workmen, a ne'er-do-well, (Heavy).Mr. Kendal.
Dutton, (Old Man) ⎰ Of the firm of Dutton & Downes, Mechan- ⎰ Mr. Clark.
Downes, (Utility) ⎱ ical Engineers and Contractors.......... ⎱ Mr. P. White.
Tollit, Sergeant of Police, (Comedy).............................Mr. Compton.
Tunks, a Prison Warder (character Comedy, Old Man)..........Mr. Rogers.
Mr. Scriven, a Stipendiary Magistrate...........................Mr. Braid.
Mould, Porter at Dutton & Co.'s................................Mr. Weathersby.
Bissett, Clerk of Court...Mr. James.
Thompson, Usher of Court.......................................Mr Johnson.
Servant..Mr. Webster.
   Policemen, Mob, &c.
Mary Warner, George's Wife (Tragedy Lead)...................Miss Bateman.
Milly Rigg, Chambermaid, afterwards Mrs. Levitt.............Miss C. Hill.
Mrs. Floyd, Landlady of No. 7 Plum Tree Court (Old Woman)...Mrs. Laws.
Mary Warner, a Child aged 7....................................Miss Mary White.
Mrs. Frenwick, Matron of Brixton Prison (Utility).............Miss Coleman.
   Female Lodgers, &c., &c.

SCENERY.

ACT. I.—*Scene* 1—Engine-builder's and iron foundry in 5th grooves.

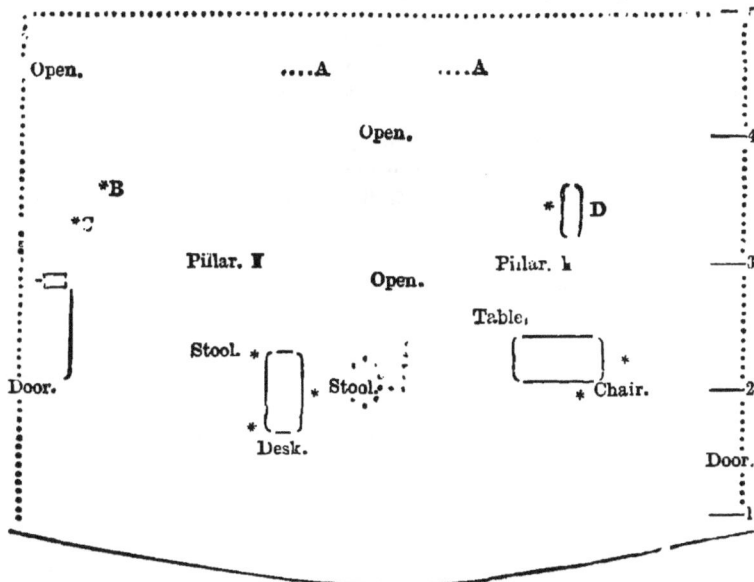

View on flat of River Thames, looking up river; St. Paul's and Houses of Parliament in the distance; London Bridge in the middle distance. 4th groove line open.
A A, in U. E., profile of river bank with anchored and grounded barges. 3d E.,
B, a steam crane; C, a steam pump, wheel to work during scene; D, engine and
driving wheel, to work during scene. 3d groove line, pillars and cross-pieces, open-
work to give view of the machinery· open at C, as a wide doorway. 1st and 2d E.,

office interior; square of carpet down c. L. and R. 3 E., open. Maps, plans, diagrams, colored lithographs of steamships, steamboats and locomotives, cut-out patterns, models of steam and hydraulic engines, hung on nails or placed about the stage. Row of hat pegs, R. 2 E. corner. High double office desk, R of c., with top rail, desk-side to lift; in left front compartment, a japanned tin cash-box; high stools for it. Borders and sink, 1st and 2d E., represent crossbeams and supports.

Scene 2—Street in 1st grooves. Scene 3—Interior in 3d grooves.

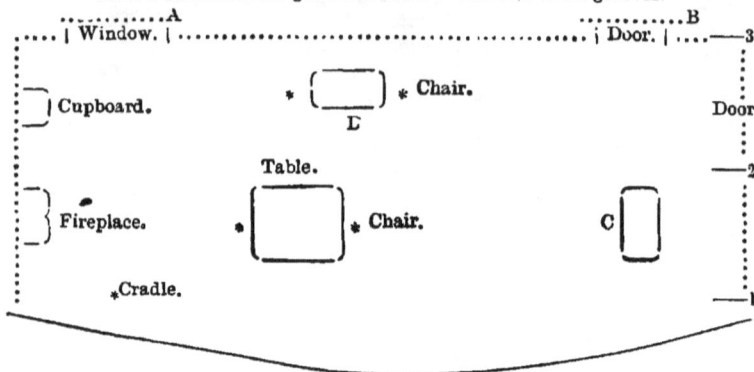

Room of a well-to-do workman; carpet down c., five yards square. A, backing to window in F., representing opposite side of street. B, backing to D. in F., dark wall. Gas down L. U. E.; gas up full R. 3. E. corner. Pictures on wall, drawings of mechanical objects plainly framed, outline patterns; ornaments on mantelpiece, a clock, flower vases, a gilt cup. C, a settee, with seat to lift up like the lid of a box, covered with chintz. D, a side-board, with writing materials on it. Curtains of chintz to window; flower-pots on window-sill. The fireplace, R. 1 E., has a kitchen range, grate in middle; oven left side with door to open; hot water boiler right side.

ACT II—*Scene 1*—Interior, plain, D. L. F. *Scene 2*—Prison interior in 6 grooves.

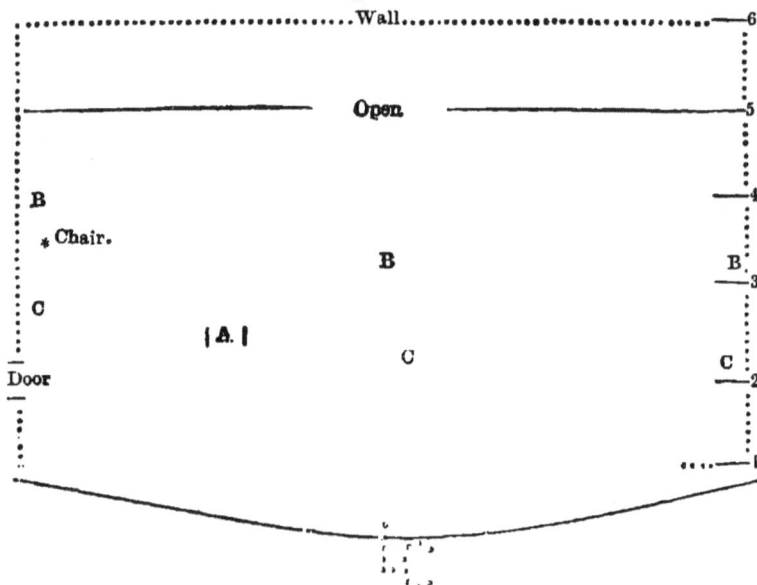

Dark sinks like large square stone wall.   Side sets, stone wall.   R. 2 F D., small grated wicket, high up in it, bolt and lock inside. Opening C., in 5th groove flat, a large doorway, the doors supposed to open all the way back into U. E., and are thus unseen from the front; open space above door barred. The lines B B and C C represent a fence, breast high, of two-inch plank, slate color, with black perpendicular stripes to look like iron uprights; black top edge as if iron rail; from B B B's, upper edge to the flies, a netting of fine wire, three-inch-square meshes. A, a door in the C. fence, which gives entrance to the R. 3 E. corner, where is a chair for the matron.

ACT III. – *Scene* 1.—Garret and view of London in 4th grooves.

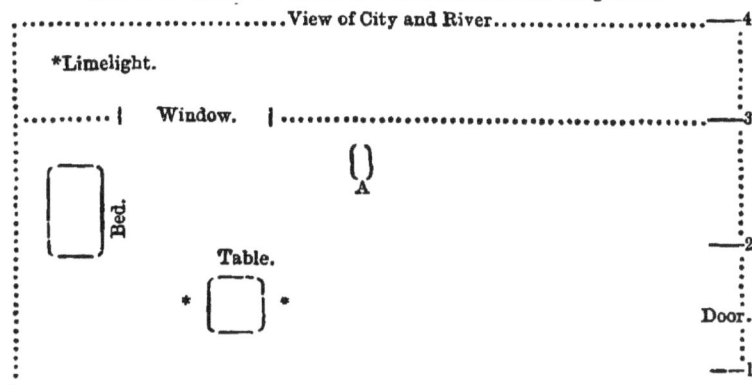

The view is by moonlight of London, the Thames, near Westminster Bridge, as from an upper-floor. Bed, R. 2 E. corner, is concealed by hangings of old and tattered chintz, hung on clothes-line. A clothes-line from O. on F. to L. 2 E., with an odd stocking or two. All the furniture poor. A, wash-basin on a stool. The window is large for moonlight effect; one curtain and a newspaper pinned on its lower panes; panes broken.

Scene 2.—Room, plain, in 1st grooves.   *Scene* 3.—Interior of Police Court in 4th grooves.   R. side the entrances open.

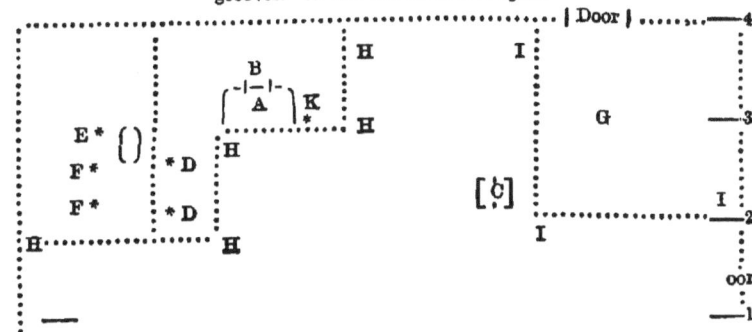

Wall on flat: A, witness stand; a sentry box, open in front, with door B, to open behind. C, the dock, a railed-in stand; rail mid-high. D D, seat for clerk of court and reporter. E, magistrate's seat and desk, on a platform raised above the stage level three feet. F F, seats. G, open space for spectators. H H, fence, mid-high. I I, fence, breast high. K, desk for writer.

ACT IV.—*Scene* 1.—An alley, winter's night effect, in 5th grooves.

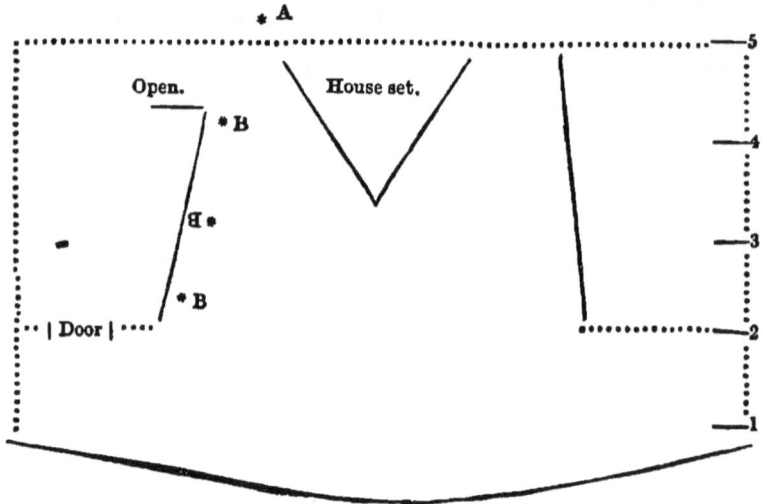

On flat, housetops of London. A, the clock tower of the Houses of Parliament. Sunset light. C. U. E., set house. Houses R. and L., very poor, old and ruined. Snow-cloth down, and snow on houses. R. 2 E., house, with three steps to door; bell-pull to door, bell to ring within. B B B, gaslamps, to light. Limelight for moonlight, L. 1 E., to throw light on R. 1 E. corner.

Scene 2.—A plain room in 1st cut, 1st grooves. A chintz curtain precisely like that of bed in Scene 1st, Act 3d hangs, L. F. as if hiding bed. Fireplace painted, R. F. *Scene* 3.—Rich interior in 2d cut of 1st grooves. *Scene* 4.—Richly furnished drawing-room in 5th grooves.

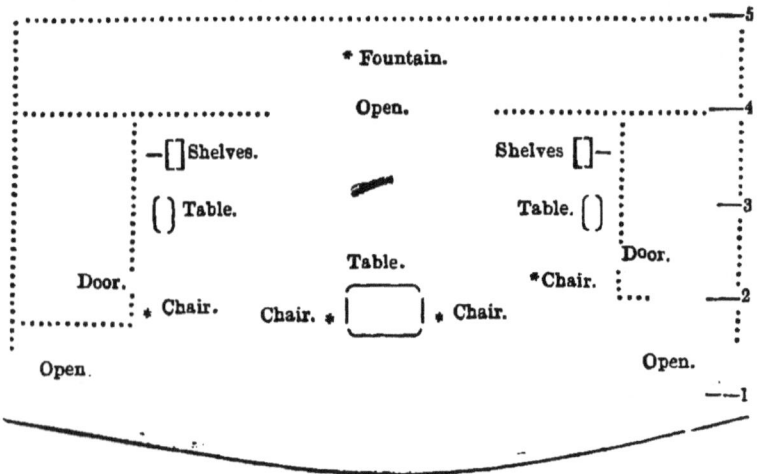

On flat, conservatory. Rich curtains to open doorway in 4th grooves, looped up each side. Shelves or etageres, R. and L. 3 E. Gaselier C. 2 E. Two large lamps, R. 2 E., on table. Fancy table L. 2 E. On shelves, R. 3 E., the gilt cup in Act I. Scene 2d. Fountain O. U. E., large, with globe of goldfish under the jet. Carpet down.

COSTUMES.

GEORGE WARNER—*Act I.*—Cloth cap, white linen jacket and overalls over dark vest and pants; shoes. Pair of compasses in jacket right-hand pocket. Chin beard and bushy side whiskers. *Act II.*—Dark blue jacket, dark vest; white overalls, clean; cap as before. *Act III.*—Walking dress, high black hat, white vest, gray pants with black cord down seam, watch-chain; beard trimmed carefully. *Act IV.*—Dark suit.

BOB LEVITT—*Act I.*—Moustache, small and carefully trimmed; gay, reckless air. Hickory shirt, black tie with fancy pin; white overalls, much blackened with iron dust; glazed cap; black jacket, hair rather long. *Act II.*—Hair and beard untrimmed and very wild. Black high hat much battered; black velvet cutaway coat, torn under the arms to show soiled white shirt; light pants, soiled. *Acts III. and IV.*—Very ragged black suit, no shirt collar; ragged handkerchief around neck. Black wideawake.

TOLLIT.—Side whiskers, or close shaven. London policeman's uniform, blue, brass buttons; two white chevrons on each sleeve, as he is a Sergeant.

TUNES.—Prison warder's uniform, a darker blue than the policeman's; frock coat; blue cloth cap with black glazed peak; pocket book with bankbills in it for *Act I.*; cane; bald on the forehead.

DUTTON.—Black coat, gray pants, white vest, high black hat.

DOWNES.—Black suit, high black hat; pocket-book and watch-chain.

SCRIVEN.—Black suit, high black hat. *Act IV.*—Evening dress.

MOULD.—Blue striped shirt, sleeves rolled up to elbow; hair tossed about carelessly; brown vest, dark pants, with blue overalls. Hands and clothes stained with iron filings and casting-sand.

BISSETT, Clerk of Court.—Plain walking suit.

THOMPSON, Usher of Court.—Long black gown with wide hanging sleeves—long rod.

SERVANT to Warner.—Dark suit.

POLICE.—Blue uniforms, helmets, clubs.

MEN FOR MOB.—Varieties of Londoners' dresses.

MARY WARNER.—Cheerful looking in *Act I.* Thereafter, cheeks hollow, no color, wearied, yet determined expression. *Act I.*—Plain white walking dress, white bonnet trimmed with blue. *Act II.*—Very plain dress, dark slate color; white cap; dark blue apron; on right arm, strip of white for the "good conduct mark." *Act III.*—Dark dress; red and black check shawl; white apron. *Act IV.*—Same.

MILLY RIGG—*Act I.*—Showy walking dress; hat with feathers and flowers; hair in curls or chignon. *Act II.*—Neat dress, hat. *Act III.*—Very poor dress hair caught up carelessly to the back of the head. *Act IV.*—Tolerably neat dress, bonnet.

MRS. FLOYD.—Cap, large pattern dress; false curls in front in the old style. *Scene 3d, Act III.*—Shawl.

MRS. FRENWICK, prison matron. — Grave, stern face, the lines of the features wired to make them prominent. Dark brown dress; bunch of keys to a chain from waistbands. Hair plain, in cap.

WOMEN FOR MOB.—In variety of London women's dresses.

MARY WARNER, a child of seven years.—White dress with sash. Hair in curls.

[For Properties and Stage Directions, see last page.]

MARY WARNER.

ACT I.

SCENE I.—*Office and Foundry in 5th grooves.*

Discover Mr. Dutton *at* L., *front end of desk,* C.

Dutton (*writing*). Yes, I think that is quite right—twenty-four pounds, four and six.

Enter, L. U. E., *and in by* C. *doorway,* Mould.

Mould. A party by app'intment, sir, wants to see you.
Dut. What's his name?
Mould. He wouldn't give any, sir.
Dut. Wouldn't give his name?

Enter, L. U. E., *and in by* C. *doorway,* Sergeant Tollit.

Tollit (*salutes*). It's about that party who is now studying the interior of the Model Prison, sir.
Dut. Oh, Mr. Tollit!   [*Exit* Mould, L. U E.
Tol. Hush! (*looks after* Mould) Never give names, sir, except to your liquor! (*comes down*) Well, sir, we have completed that case all snug. (*comes round to* R. C.) The fellow was readily found guilty.
Dut. After a deal of trouble.
Tol. The trouble's a pleasure. You furnished the information, I nobble the party, and there's the end of it.
Dut. Not quite the end of it, Mr. Tollit, for I wish to pay you some reward—you deserve reward.
Tol. Well, sir, I've done my duty. "England expects every man to do his duty"— but I never heard it was to be done for nothing!
Dut. Right! what is duty for but to be paid! (*takes bankbill from cash-box*) There you are, Mr. Tollit. (*gives bill to* Tollit) And I never paid away a fiver with more pleasure in all my life. The fellow would have still gone on plundering us but for you.
Tol. Thank you, sir. (*pockets note*) This thieving by clerks is going on in more large places of business than anyone out of the police suspects. It's lucky that your articles here are so heavy—castings are not as light as cash-boxes.
Dut. I don't know. Our chaps require a deal of looking after. We have to turn out things so cheap that the pick of men won't work for us. I don't like contract work, as I always tell Mr. Downes.

Tol. Oh, sir, I daresay there is a deal of robbery going on.

Dut. We mean to stick more to the instrument making. Let others use them in manufactures; what men want is tools, tools, sir.

Tol. A pretty general want, sir.

Dut. Why, there's nothing that can't be produced if only the material and implements are found I don't despair of seeing a steam police some day. Ha, ha! Wind 'em up to go on the principle of an eight-day clock.

Tol. (*imitating striking a blow with club with ruler taken off desk*). Not forgetting the striking movement, ha, ha.

Dut. Ha, ha, not bad.

Enter, l. u. e., *and in by* c., Bob Levitt, *with a bag of tools and a metal faucit in his hand.*

Dut. Well, what do you want? (*scarcely looks at* Levitt. Tollit *gives* Levitt *one glance, and then looks round carelessly*) Oh! the working model. (*takes the faucit from* Levitt) It's a new improvement in sugar-mill machinery—(*to* Tollit) one of our men gave us the first idea of it, and we have patented it. He grumbles about it, I believe. Ah! there's no getting on with the working classes now-a-days! They have all heard of the claims of labor, ha, ha. (*moves the metal screw head, etc*) Are you any judge of such things, Mr. Tollit! (Tollit *shakes his head;* Curious, this slot and the valve-joint. (*goes to table up* l, *takes up rule, applies it to faucit*) Yes, yes—halloa! Let me see! there's something wrong here! (*measures with rule*) one—two—four—five—yes! (*to* Levitt) Do you call that true to guage? Look at the valve! pshaw! You have spoilt the whole of it by your bungling. Do you call yourself a workman? When you take your wages on pay day, you need not come here again?

Lev. Don't say that, sir. Give a fellow another chance.

Dut. (*looks at him*). Oh! (*lays metal on* l. *table*) It is Bob Levitt, is it? I might have guessed as much by the work. Mr. Bob Levitt, you were evidently planned out for a play-actor, and not an engineer. As you go back, tell George Warner I want to see him. (Levitt *retires up* l. c., *disconsolately*) Is there anything else I can do for you, Mr. Tollit? (*goes* l. *with* Tollit) May be you would like to look around the works while you are here?

Tol. Thank you, sir, I'm what they call a—a—a *cunnin'-seer* of tools —it's quite amazing the march of intellect in roguery. We have made an astonishing advance in tools. Did you ever see a first-rate jack-in-the-box?

Dut. (*laughs*). Really, Mr. Tollit, you must ask my children that?

Tol. Oh! I mean the tool and not the toy. A cracksman will have tools that don't stand in need of finish. A "lagger" don't lag behind in the march. It's the effects of scientific eddication. But when a new idea comes to brains, *we* have them first, and I'm down on the thieves like—like your steam hammer there.

Dut. Ah! there's a fine invention—it suits everything—from forging a crank to cracking a nut.

Tol. Well, sir, I don't know much about forging a crank, but cracking a *nut* is quite in my line. (*he directs* Dutton's *attention to his not closing the desk drawer, and* Dutton *locks it. They go* l., *and exeunt* l. d., *in conversation.*)

Lev. (*comes down* l. c., *looks to* l. d.). Go along with you, you hard-hearted old rhinoceros! And soft-headed, too. If it hadn't been for the bobby you would have left the cash-box out, and Bob Levitt might have helped himself to the wages you owe him. "Heaven helps them that helps themselves "—that's a good copybook head. And why not? Who is going to help Bob Levitt now that he has got the sack? Bah! (c.) I wasn't born for this dull work. (*in deep contempt*) Engineering! engineering! *mechanical* engineer! not even *civil!* I always wanted to cut it, and now I am obliged to old Dutton for the shake-off. I ought to be a master myself and order everybody around. All I want is capital. I've got the style, a handsome bearing, a rich voice, an easy manner—all one wants to be an ornament to society. (*goes to desk*) There's the wings to fly with! Ah! if he had only left the key in the lock. (*about to try to force desk open, turns, looks to L. U. E.*) Hullo! here comes —(*goes up*) old Downes. He must not see me here. (*goes R.*) I will go into the washing-room. They never goes there—the dirty beggars! (*with scorn*) they never washes their hands, the low fellows!

                                        [*Exit,* R. D.

Enter, R. U. E., *and on by* C. D., DOWNES, *followed by* TUNKS. DOWNES *comes to* L. *front end of desk, and* TUNKS *marches down* L. C., *around to* R. C., *and takes stool by desk*

DOWNES. Take a chair, Mr. Tunks, (TUNKS *seats himself*) while I make out the receipt. (TUNKS *sponges his face with handkerchief*) Forty-one pounds, six and eightpence. (*writes, while* TUNKS *gets banklills ready.*)

TUNKS (*giving bills*). And a very neat job you made of that last order —the grating for the visiting cell is most excellent. That was a clever young fellow you sent to put it up.

DOWNES. Oh, George Warner? (*puts bills in cash-box in desk, which he unlocks with his key.*)

TUNKS. Yes.

DOWNES. Yes, he's clever, but wrong-headed. He has fallen to reading the papers, and has got filled with stuff about the Rights of Labor, Co-operation and all the like—evil ideas. Let the workmen once get a finger in the pie and they won't leave much for capital.

TUNKS (*laughing*). There wouldn't be many plums left in the pie, ha, ha! (*puts receipt up.*)

DOWNES (*closes desk*). Well, shall I see you out?

TUNKS. Thank you. (*they go up* C.) Good-morning!

DOWNES. Good-morning.   [*Exit with* TUNKS, C. D. *and* R. U. E.

Enter, R. D., LEVITT, *to* C.

LEV. Right you are, old man! Here's one of your workmen who is going in for his snacks. (*goes to desk*) He's left the key in—Ah! (*vexed*) more interruptions!   [*Exit,* R. D.

Enter, L. U. E., *and on by* C. D., GEORGE WARNER. *Enter,* L. D., DUTTON

DUT. Ah, George! Didn't Levitt tell you that I wanted to see you!

WAR. No, sir. (*cap on.*)

DUT. Oh! he's gone off in the sulks. (*gives metal model*) Just look at that sugar-mill, George, and see what a precious bungle Levitt has made of it. Only see that valve. (C.) Ah! you've found it out!

WAR. Oh, there's no mistake about it. (*up* L. C.)

DUT. (*at desk*). No mistake? It's all mistakes!

WAR. That's what I meant, sir.

DUT. It must be made over again.

WAR. I say, sir——

DUT. What is it?

WAR. Wouldn't it save power if—(*stops.*)

DUT. What? (*eagerly.*)

WAR. (*gravely*). After all, it's no business of mine. I'll follow the pattern, and that's enough.

DUT. George, you see your way to some improvement in this?

WAR. Well, sir, I think I do. But the idea may be of some good to me, yet.

DUT. Come, come, I like to encourage inventive talent. Downes laughed at that man with the new slotting movement, but I bought it——

WAR. Yes, you bought it, and patented it in your own name. (*musing-ly*) It must have brought you in a deal of profit.

DUT. But your idea?

WAR. No! that reminder is a lesson for me to keep my idea to myself.

DUT. But one of these days you will be a master yourself, and one of your workmen may come to you with an idea, which you will patent——

WAR. (*firmly*). Then I will give him a share of the profit.

DUT. (*shocked*). Oh! Ah, this comes of your co-operative nonsense. What can you do with an idea which you haven't the capital to put into form?

WAR. Take it with me to a country where a man can get free space to do what he likes with his own.

DUT. George, speak out! Don't be a fool!

WAR. I won't be one again! Mr. Dutton, you have no one in your employ whom you have done better by than me.

DUT. There's not a man in the shop whom I esteem so much as you.

WAR. (*hotly*). There's twenty whom you give better wages than me! I'm tired of it. Me and Mary have been talking the matter over, and we have made up our minds to go abroad.

DUT. Go abroad? You will repent it, George.

WAR. Then I will come back again. But (*bashfully*) I don't like to go out with only what I stand up in—would you mind advancing me twenty pounds? (*cap in hand.*)

DUT. Not to cut your own throat! I think too much of you for that. (*pause.*) But I'll tell you what I will do. I'll give you a five-pound note for your idea.

WAR. (*puts cap on*). No! you keep your five pounds, and I'll keep my idea, Mr. Dutton. Five pounds! pah! if I had my share of all I have earned for you, Mr. Dutton, all that is in that box wouldn't equal it, ten times over!

DUT. (*sneers*). Perhaps you had better help yourself!

WAR. No! I don't want to help myself—not that that would be more than my right. I want you to pay me my just share of profits—that would start me in a new country.

Enter, L. U. E. *to* C., MOULD.

MOULD. Mr. Downes wants to see you, sir.

DUT. Tell him I will be with him directly. (*Exit* MOULD, L. U. E.) Well, think it over, George. (*closes drawer and leaves key in*) Don't do what you will repent. (*to* L. U. E.) I'll soon be back. [*Exit.*

WAR. (*alone*). There! I told Mary how it would be. And Dutton's the best of the two. This is how he treats me!—me that's made many a twenty pound for him! He says I will repent. Well, maybe I will—but it won't be because he did not oblige me. I'm sorry I ever asked him. I can find work anywhere—Mary will carry the happiness of our little home along with us, and our little girl will never know what our life threatened to be before we took up our dwelling abroad. So, good-bye, Dutton & Downes! leaving you is the best day's work I ever did for myself—may it be a lesson for you not to drive away the very bearers and supports of your house. [*Exit, R. U. E. by C. D.*

Enter, R. D. to C., cautiously, LEVITT.

LEVITT. Bravo Oh, them hounds that don't think an honest workman is worth his salt. I'll help myself to my share—old Dutton has left open the salt-box. (*whistles as he lays his hand on desk, L., front end*) As we say in the shop—the metal is all ready to cut and run! (*about to open desk*) Hark! here's a stoppage! [*Exit, R. D.*

Enter, L. U. E., and on by C. D., MARY WARNER, *followed by* MOULD.

MOULD (*up L. C.*). They've just gone out, Mrs. Warner, but one or t'other of them will be back presently. Shall I tell George you are here?

MRS. WARNER. No! I have my reasons.

MOULD. You always have your reasons, Mrs. Warner. I say to my young woman that that's where you differ from other young women—they never have any reasons. [*Exit, C. D. and L. U. E.*

MRS. W. I am glad I did not meet George as I came in—I cannot wish to see him now. I came along so hopeful, but somehow my heart sinks now I am here. I know what his modesty is—he shrinks from asking anything like a favor, or not the exact due of what he has earned. It's my duty to spare him all I can, and a request like this may come from a woman's mouth. (R. C. *by desk*) Yet I don't like it! Courage! Better that I than he, should ask them for what George calls his rights. (*leans one hand on stool* R. C.)

Enter, L. D., DUTTON.

DUT. (*cheerfully*). My dear Mrs. Warner, how do you do? (*to desk, looks around*) Where is George? I left him here not a moment ago, and told him to wait.

MRS. W. There was no one here when I came, and I am glad of it. I did not want George to know I came here.

DUT. Oh! a secret from your husband?

MRS. W. Except by the result of my visit, I wish George not to know of it. I came to spare him trouble. I wish to ask you to lend us twenty pounds, as we are going to the United States, and want money in case of ill luck at first.

DUT. That's what George spoke to me about when he was here not a minute ago. I couldn't let so good a hand go off on a wild goose chase. Still, I offered him five pounds for an idea of his, which shows I had no ill feeling. But he is full of that communism, socialism and co-operation nonsense. I hope you will talk to him and bring him back to his senses.

MRS. W. After all he has done for you in this place, you won't help us on our way to the New World?

DUT. I should never forgive myself if I did. Come, look at it seriously. Isn't the five pounds in the hand better than any amount in the bush ? Ah ! you will see it soberly. You don't fire up like George. You take things differently from him, I see.

MRS. W. (*shakes her head*). No; I knew what it would cost him to ask that favor, but I did not know till now what it was to be refused. (*going up c.*)

DUT. No; I'll not let you go away in anger like that, Mrs. Warner. I esteem you and George too highly to lose you. He and I parted in a bit of a quarrel—he said that I owed him ten times what money I had here, and I don't like high words—it put up my dander, I can tell you. Now you talk to him soothingly, and make him see that it would be better for him to take the five pounds, and stay where he is ; you take the money—say, it is for baby——

MRS. W. No! what he didn't think was enough for him, I *know* was too little. Thank you, I'd rather not.

DUT. Well, I never knew the equal of you as an obstinate couple. I'll send George in here to you, and that will make you each ashamed of the other.

MRS. W. No ; fifty times five pounds couldn't do that, sir.

Enter, L. U. E. to c., MOULD.

MOULD (*tucking up his shirt-sleeves, already rolled up to the elbow*). They are going to run that great spur-wheel, sir !

DUT. Very well; I'm a-coming. (*Exit* MOULD *quickly,* L. U. E.) Wait till you see me. Think it over. You'll think better of it. I won't be long. [*Exit,* L. U. E.

MRS. W. (*alone*). He says I will think better of it! (*smiles contemptuously*) Shall I wait till George comes ? (*goes up*) No, better that I should go without his knowing that I ever came. That's the man that George has given the best of his young years to, and yet he refuses to fill his hand—aye, with what he has earned over and over again. Wait till he returns! not I! I'll work my fingers to the bone before I would ask his help again ! [*Exit,* C. D. *and* R. U. E.

Enter, R. D., LEVITT,

LEV. Ha! It was lucky I had to bolt back ! Here's a touching story for my gentle ears ! To go and refuse twenty pounds to a man that has made hundreds for them—the misers ! (*to desk*) I'll give them twenty-five out of the haul, before they shall be done out of their rights. The key's forgotten. (*opens desk and gets cash-box*) Easy done ! and nobody the wiser. (*puts box in his tool bag, which he shoulders*) I've done a good day's work—I'll go home and go to bed ! [*Exit,* C. D. *and* R. U. E.

Enter, L. D., DUTTON, DOWNES *and* TOLLIT. TOLLIT *up* L. C., DUTTON *to* L. *front end of desk, and* DOWNES *to* R. *side of desk.*

DUT. Oh, she has gone, then.

DOWNES. Who's that ?

DUT. George Warner's wife. She's off in a huff, because I refused him a loan.

DOWNES. Of course, you refused ?

DUT. Of course, and I told his wife that it was foolishness to leave a good place to overstock America. Bless you, all the foresight and carefulness of business men is on this side of the water.

DOWNES. Beyond doubt.

TOL. Of course, sir. Oh, Mr. Dutton, some one's left the key in the drawer.

DOWNES. Eh! it wasn't me—(*sees that he has his key*)—by the way, Dutton, I've put that payment in, the Brixton Prison job—you'll find it all right.

DUT. (*opens drawer*) Hullo! I say Downes!

DOWNES. What! had a stroke?

DUT. It's gone!

TOL. }
DOWNES. } What's gone?

DUT. The cash-box!

DOWNES. The devil!

TOL. If parties will leave keys in parties' drawers, other parties will turn them! It's human nature. Let's look at the matter calmly. Who put money in last?

DOWNES. I did, not a quarter of an hour ago.

TOL. Now then to discover who took out. You put in. Who has been in the office?

DUT. Only George Warner and his wife. I left each in the office alone.

TOL. That's the clue. Who did it—let's toss up! "Man or woman?"

Scene changes to

SCENE II.—*Street in 1st groov*

Enter, R., MRS. WARNER. *Enter* MILLY RIGG, L., *to meet*, R. C.

MRS. W. What! Milly Rigg!

MILLY. Mary Warner! (*they shake hands and kiss*) I have not seen you for so long!

MRS. W. Oh, Milly! how gay you are!

MIL. And how shabby you look! How's baby, and what's made you look so down in the mouth. Where have you been keeping yourself, you bad old girl.

MRS. W. I have been very busy at home with baby and my husband.

MIL. Oh! certainly. Have you heard of my good luck?

MRS. W. (*sadly*). That you have found a husband?

MIL. And you don't congratulate me? Oh! I see! You never forget that Bob Levitt paid you attentions.

MRS. W. It is not that.

MIL. I suppose then that your husband sets you against him?

MRS. W. I never loved Bob Levitt.

MIL. Of course not! Pooh! don't be a goose. Why shouldn't we be married?

MRS. W. I don't object. What right have I to interfere, though I only care to ensure your happiness?

MIL. Don't say that? Who got me a situation when I was out of work—who spent her Sundays a-nursing me when I was ill—and gave me so much good advice that I don't make any use of? (*presses* MRS. WARNER'S *hand.*)

MRS. W. Ah, Milly, you are light-spirited, but you have a good, kind, loving heart. That's why I want only a deserving man to have such a treasure. I wish that was soon. I shall leave you with a heavy heart, if you are not well wedded before we have gone to America.

MIL. Going away?

MRS. W. To America. George is tired of the life he leads here. He

says there is no chance for a man that is down but wants to rise. He
has given notice to Dutton & Downes of his leaving. By the way, I
have news for you from there—but, no——

MIL. Is it bad news? It is not of Bob? what?

MRS. W. I wish I hadn't to say it. He is discharged.

MIL. Oh! (*then, lightly*) Pooh! there's plenty of shops as good as
Dutton & Downes'. He won't have to go far without finding a door
open.

MRS. W. But they won't give him a character, I hear.

MIL. (*tauntingly*). Did George have nothing good to say for this old
lover of yours?

MRS. W. George had no chance to speak for him. Ah, Milly, Bob
does not like work—he is much too fond of pleasure.

MIL. What do you expect of the young? Why shouldn't we go
ahead? I'm fond of pleasure—we are both fond of pleasure. I am
not going to be a nun, for anybody that I know. When *are* we to have
our fling? (*very gayly*) But Bob is waiting for me. We are going to the
theatre, and then hie for Cremorne and a dance on the crystal platform.
(*dances while singing* "la, la, la" *to a popular waltz tune*) Oh! he's the
loveliest partner, Bob is!

MRS. W. Oh, Milly, don't!

MIL. Partner in the lancers, partner in life!

MRS. W. No, Milly. He is not the man for a wife who thinks of
pleasure first, and business afterwards. The time will come soon when
you will hunger for what you now waste.

MIL. Time enough to make bread when it is wanted. For my part I
don't see what there is against Bob, and my being Mrs. Levitt. Where's
the harm. He's got all the accomplishments! He sings a good song,
and he polks divinely. What they call an A 1 swell! If he was in a
higher sphere, he would be voted a tip-top ornament to society.

MRS. W. Aye, Milly, if he were in a higher sphere, his gifts might be
prizes to him, but what has a working man to do with such things. Well
for him if he can live from day to day, with one continual effort of self-
devotion. George often says that a working man must not think of luxuries.

MIL. Pooh! we will do without the necessaries of life in order to
have the luxuries. We shall do together, never fear. If butterflies do
only enjoy the summer, what matter? isn't that the best of the year?
But I am keeping Bob waiting for me——

MRS. W. No!—don't go. Nay, you shall not leave me. Something
tells me that no good will result from your intimacy with that man.
You know how light and fickle he is, and how seldom he is at home.
Come with me, dear, and I will show you what home with a happy husband really is—a welcome always at the door and peace and deep con-
tent within. (MILLY *struggles with her, both going* L.)

MIL. But I can't break my appointment.

MRS —. Only for once. Do come.   [*They exeunt* L.

Scene changes to

SCENE III.—*Interior of dwelling house in 3d grooves.*

Enter, D. *in* F., BOB LEVITT.

LEVITT (*comes down* C., *with cash-box brought out from under his coat*).
There is no one here. George and Mary not come home yet. They
will little suspect who has been here in their absence. An angel's visit

—" doing good by stealth "—and afraid to say anything about it. (*gets chisel*) Here's one of George's tools—I wonder if it will fit. (*breaks open cash-box*) The trick's done! notes—gold! Whew! here's a nest of gold-finches! (*whistles*) And a heap of notes that they've been pillowed on. (*counts bank-bills*) Five—ten—twenty—twenty-five—thirty—sixty—(*mumbles the rest indistinctly*) two hundred and fifty pounds, by Jove! sinking the small change! (*rises from stooping over box on table c.*) This is something like a morning's work! Now to help this young couple on their venture to America. Bob Levitt always keeps his word. (*counts bank-bills*) Five, five—ten—twenty and five. Right! I'll wrap it up in a bit of paper. (*gets paper*) What's this? (*reads*) " List of steamers sailing to the United States." Blank the other side—that'll do. (*folds bills in paper*) Where's pen and ink? (*gets pen and ink from sideboard up c.*) I'll write my name on the back—(*stops his hand*) no, I won't, neither. (*writes*) " From an unknown benefactor." They'll think it comes from old Dutton. (*quickly, laughing*) And so it does, too. (*fills his pockets with bills and coin*) What shall I do with the cash-box? (*looks round*) Oh! the sofa—the lid lifts up—(*opens settee, L.*)—in the well is the place. (*puts box inside settee*) When they have gone, I can buy this in when their sticks are sold off. Till then, let *well* alone. (*closes settee top, and goes up c.*) Now I am off. (*opens D. F., but closes it instantly*) There's somebody coming up stairs. They've come home. I'll run up stairs—I hate gratitude.   [*Exit D. F. A pause, stage clear.*

Enter, D. F., MRS. WARNER *and* MILLY RIGG, *coming down c.*

MRS. W. Here we are. George is not in yet. I'm glad of it. I don't like him to find me out, and nothing ready for him. Take off your things. (MILLY *loosens strings of her hat, etc., but need not remove it;* MRS. WARNER *gets apron within* L. D.) Now, Milly, (*ties on apron; leads* MILLY *to cradle* R., *front*) I'll show you the great attraction of the establishment.

MIL. What's that?
MRS. W. The baby! (*business at cradle.*)
MIL. Oh, I forgot!
MRS. W. I wouldn't show it to everybody.
MIL. Oh, my! what a little thing it is!
MRS. W. Little! it's very big for its age! it's a lovely baby
MIL. Ah! I don't see much of it—I can only see its eyes!
MRS. W. Isn't it lovely, now?
MIL. It's opening its mouth! what does it say?
MRS. W. Pshaw! it can't speak!
MIL. Oh, how stupid! But then I don't know much about babies.
MRS. W. (*takes gilt cup from mantle shelf*). Isn't that nice?
MIL. (*carelessly*). It is pretty.
MRS. W. (*indignantly*). Pretty! It is splendid! Do you see them? (*points to pictures.*)
MIL. (*looks round*). The what?
MRS. W. The drawings—George did them all—they are wonderful, aint they? and all out of his own head! I don't understand them, but they are so good. They are mechanical.
MIL. (*looks at drawing*). Is that a dahlia or a pigeon?
MRS. W. For shame, Milly. What an idea! (*both at c.*, MILLY *on her left*) How snug and how nice a home! Really, Milly, I don't know how I can ever leave it for a new one abroad.
MIL. Don't! stay with us! (MRS. W. *lays table, spreads cloth, etc.*)

Can't I help you? I may be going to housekeeping myself soon, and then I may be glad to have learnt.

MRS. W. Oh, you may. (MILLY *helps her to set table*) Here, put the tea-pot on the hob to draw.

MIL. Should I drop it?

MRS W. Don't, for George wouldn't forgive you, though I did. (MILLY *puts tea-pot* R. 1 E.

MIL. If you were'nt going away, it would be so nice for me to come every day for a lesson. (*takes up milk jug*) Is this to go on the fire, too?

MRS. W. Bless us, no! Come sit you down, and let me go on with the rest myself.

MIL. Are you sure I am not in the way? (*seated* L. *of table.*)

MRS. W. (*arranging things on table*). You are in the right way, dear.

MIL How quick you are, Mary, and how neat.

MRS. W. (*smiles*). Oh! it wasn't always so. I shall never forget the first dinner I made for George after we were married. It was all spoilt, and the beef was burned to a coal (*laughs*). I daresay he thought he had got a bad bargain. But I have improved wonderfully since my first start.

MIL. There was no room for improvement.

MRS. W. (*suddenly, after glancing* R.). Milly, do you like beefsteak pie?

MIL. (*enthusiastically*). I adore beefsteak pie!

MRS. W. Because I have made one. (MILLY *rises*) And you may take it out of the oven if you like.

MIL. (*goes* R.). It's the first time I ever did such a thing in my life. (*in opening oven door, burns her fingers, goes to* C., *business of shaking her hand, putting it to her lips, etc.*) Oh!

MRS. W. (*half laughing*). Poor Milly! has she hurt her poor fingers!

MIL. A beefsteak pie may be a very nice thing, but it is awfully hot. (MRS. W. *takes pie from oven with a holder*) Oh! you did not tell me of that.

MRS. W. I thought everybody knew that much.

MIL. Thanks for the lesson. I'll have it at my fingers end hereafter, long enough. (MRS. W. *puts pie on table*) What, aint you going to give baby a piece of pie?

MRS. W. What a horrible idea!

MIL. It will keep it quiet.

MRS. W. (*to cradle*). Keep it quiet—a dear diamond duck of a quiet baby that it is!

MIL. (*hides her face in her hands and sobs*). Oh!

MRS. W. (*goes to her*). Oh! Milly, what's the matter? (*takes her head in her hands and soothes her.*)

MIL. Nothing, nothing, (*tearfully*) but the seeing you so happy in your happy little home, makes me feel what a bad, wicked, useless girl I am!

MRS. W. Not useless, Milly. You are too good not to have such a home yourself.

MIL. Don't praise me—don't pity me! I don't deserve it!

MRS. W. There are none of us that deserve good fortune; we can only try.

MIL. I never can hope for it.

MRS. W. Oh! dry your eyes. (*bell* L.). Here's George! he mustn't see you in tears! He sees nothing but smiles here! (MILLY *rises*; MRS. WARNER *goes up to* D. F.) There are two—he has brought some one with him. No! it is not his step! (*as* D. F. *opens, she recedes down* L. C.)

Enter, D. F., DOWNES *and* DUTTON, *who come down* R. *side to front. Enter, same,* TOLLIT.*

MRS. W. Mr. Dutton? (*puzzled.*)

DUT. George not home yet?

MRS. W. He has not come in yet. What do you want with him.

DUT. I'd rather not say before third parties. (*indicating* MILLY.)

DOWNES. Who is that?

MRS. W. That's Miss Rigg—a friend of mine, and George's. You can say anything you have got to say before her. I am not ashamed of George, and I know he is not ashamed of me.

TOL. Better let me speak, gentlemen. The sooner we get it out, the sooner the young woman will get over it. The fact is, it's a small matter of robbery.

MIL. Robbery!

MRS. W. Robbery, and my George! (*deep unbelief.*)

Enter, D. F., WARNER, *throws his cap* L. *and comes down* L. C., *whistling lightly; when about to embrace* MRS. WARNER, *sees* DUTTON.

WAR. Mr. Downes! and Mr. Dutton! (*sees* TOLLIT, *with contempt*) What does *he* want here? (MRS. WARNAR *clings to him.*)

DUT. George, we have missed something from the office——

MRS. W. And they suspect you of taking it——

DUT. Only he and you were in the place at the time.

WAR. Why, she has not been near your office!

DUT. Oh, yes, she has.

MRS. W. It is true.

WAR. And you never told me?

MRS. W. I meant to spare you the pain of a refusal, George, though I did not know then how painful it would be.

WAR. Well, what of it? Because an honest man asked his employers to lend him a few pounds, is he to have his home broken into by policemen like this?

DUT. It is not that, George.

WAR. What then? Is it some lie trumped up to bind a man down here when he wants to go to a country where a working man is not exposed to being intruded into like this.

DUT. George, you and your wife, were left alone in our office, where the cash-box was, in an open drawer. You knew where it was, and what it was, for you said to me that it contained money that you had earned, and twenty times as much!

WAR. So I did, and so it is.

TOL. Better not say any more. It may be used against you.

WAR. Better *your* bad word than your good. Out of my house (MRS. WARNER *and* MILLY *cling to him*) or I'll smash you, policeman though you are.

TOL. You see, gentlemen, I was right when I said we had better have help at hand. (*blows whistle*) Easy does it. No violence, my man.

Enter, D. F., TWO POLICEMEN.

Look there! (MRS. WARNER *faints in* MILLY'S *and* WARNER'S *arms*) The young woman is took bad.

---

* TOLLIT.*
DUTTON.*
DOWNES.*

* MILLY.
* MRS. WARNER.

WAR. This is my reward for all I have done for you (*looks at* DUTTON) and him. (*looks at* DOWNES.)

DUT. I'm sorry for you, George. This comes of giving way to all the wild schemes of co-operation and taking possession of " your own."

WAR. (*fiercely*). How dare you accuse me of taking your dirty money ?

TOL. It's two to one against you. Begin your search. (*to the* POLICE-MEN) There hasn't been time to hide anything. (1st POLICEMAN *finds notes in paper on side-board up* C. *and gives to* TOLLIT) What have we here ? Notes—the notes. Which of you gentlemen took the number of the notes. (DOWNES *gives him a paper*) Do they run to tally ? Beyond a doubt. Here's five of them any how ! (*general emotion.*)

WAR. Five of the notes here?

TOL. Is this chisel yours ? (*chisel taken up from table.*)

WAR. Yes.

TOL. (*examines chisel*). This is the instrument the box was opened with. (*to* POLICE) Look for the cash-box—it can't be far off. (2d POLICEMAN *finds cash-box*, L)

MRS. W. (*aside, looking at* WARNER *suspiciously*). This is the first time that I have been ashamed for him. (2d POLICEMAN *gives* TOLLIT *the cash-box.*)

WAR. What proof have you ? Get out of my house !

TOL. Empty ! of course. Stand at the door ! (*to* 1st POLICEMAN) Here is the proof. It's a complete case. (*general consternation*) Parties left alone in parties' office—parties' cash-box missing—parties says that the money was their own by rights—cash-box found in parties' room, with parties' chisel to fit parties' cash-box. Now then, which of you gentlemen gives him in charge ?

MRS. W. George! George ! (*aside*) He won't speak. (*aloud*) Stop ! he is innocent !

TOL. Oh, of course, *you* will swear to it !

DUT. Then, who did it ?

MRS. W. (*wildly and powerfully*). Take me away, for it was I I

MIL. ⎱ You !
WAR. ⎰

DUT. She !

ALL *form picture.*

<pre>
                                    * POLICEMAN.
                    * DOWNES.   * 2ND POLICEMAN.
* DUTTON.   * TOLLIT.   * MRS. WARNER.   * WARNER.   * MILLY.
</pre>

CURTAIN.

ACT II.

SCENE I.—*Room in* 1st *grooves.*

Enter, L., MILLY *and* TUNKS.

MIL. (*to* R. C.). Come in, Mr. Tunks. (*gets her sewing* R) Here's my little room I thank you very much for seeing me home. Shan't I get you something?

TUNKS (L. C.). No, thank you. I never take anything before dinner.

MIL. Won't you take a chair, at least?

TUNKS. Ah! that won't get into my head. (*chuckles, seats himself* L. c.) You see, my dear, I have grown-up daughters of my own and I wouldn't like to let them walk alone all the way from Brixton, and they are neither as young nor as pretty as you, my dear! meaning no offence, my dear.

MIL. It's such a good protection to have your arm, sir.

TUNKS. Yes, there's not much to fear with me.

MIL. Only to think, though, that when I first went to visit Mary Warner in the prison, you quite frightened me.

TUNKS. I am glad of it.

MIL. (*surprised*). Glad of it?

TUNKS. Yes. You see, my dear, we prison authorities have to cultivate an air that will strike terror into the evil-doers.

MIL. You are kind enough to be my father.

TUNKS. I wish I was, and happy and proud I would be of it. Such well-conducted girls are rare. Ah! it's a consolation to know that we have our rules and regulations for us while we are on duty; and when we are off, we have one rule : " Do as you would be done by."

MIL. You dear, kind, old man, I have a great mind to give you a great big kiss.

TUNKS. Don't balk your inclination, my dear. I have daughters of my own, and I am used to it.

MIL. (*kisses him*). That's for being so kind to me. (*kisses him*) And that's for being so kind to Mary Warner.

TUNKS. Ah! it would be hard not to be kind to her, poor soul! It's a hard trial for her, but bravely she bears it. Why, she has done more good in that there prison than a ton of tracts. I often wonder how she could ever have taken that cash-box. I wouldn't believe it unless she had confessed it.

MIL. I'll not believe it. No; not if all the policemen in London swore to it till they were as blue as their coats.

TUNKS. Mr. Tollit told me as how it was the prettiest piece of circumstantial evidence as ever was heard in the Central Criminal Court. It's my belief the devil was at her elbow when she did it. The old gentleman is sometimes let off duty down below to have his diversion up here.

MIL. It's so unfortunate! her happy home broken up, her little one motherless, and her husband lonely. And only because she helped herself when those that ought to have behaved better, refused what would have been only a drop in the bucket. It was the stinginess of Dutton & Downes that caused it all——

TUNKS No, my dear. Pity her, if you will, but don't excuse her, not before one of the authorities.

MIL. I won't excuse her husband. George has not been to see her since she was in, has he?

TUNKS. Ah! that's like the women. There's no cruelty to you so dreadful as desertion. There's many a woman in our place whose husband never comes to ask after her, but there's no man whose wife doesn't come on the visiting-day, as punctual as the clock. Ah, my dear, your hearts are larger than ours, though your heads are smaller! It's hard upon her, though, to be shunned by him, when she probably only committed the theft in the idea of helping her husband.

MIL. I have written to him. He shall go and see her!

TUNKS. I hope he will. (*rises*) She deserves that comfort if ever a prisoner did Well, good-by, my dear. I will tell her anything you have to tell her.

MIL. I have nothing worth your taking, Mr. Tunks—only my love.

TUNKS. That's the best thing I could take to her, next to her husband.

MIL. Heaven bless you for all your kindness to her. You are only too good to her and me. Won't you call on Monday, and have a cup of tea? (*going* L. *with* TUNKS.)

TUNKS. Monday? Monday? I am engaged Monday, but I can come Tuesday, and come I will.

MIL. Thank you. Good-by!

TUNKS. Good-by!   [*Exit*, L.

MIL. (*returns to* C.). Poor Mary! It is certainly hard for her to be left alone by him whom she has most right to expect to come to cheer her, while her only friends are strangers. Only to think of the good advice that she gave me only the last time before she went away. It was well I followed it, for nothing good would have come to me by my sharing the shifting fortunes of that wretch Bob Levitt. He's gone off on the tramp—I wish I had him here, I'd tramp him. I hope I shall never see him again. (*knock*, L. D.) Who's that? Bob! Come in!

Enter WARNER, L., *dejected in look.*

Oh! George Warner! I am glad to see you. So you got my note?

WAR. (*sadly*). Yes, Milly, I got your letter. Thank you.

MIL. I knew you must be lonely—

WAR. I am very lonely——

MIL. Then what must she be with no one to see her.

WAR. (*takes seat* C.). I have often thought of that these six months we have been apart. My dear Mary! At the time when you were gone to see her, I have been imagining how she looked, and I have fancied myself with her. How I wanted to hear what she was saying to you.

MIL. How she longs to see you—how she talks of the love she bears for you!

· WAR. Mine has grown for her as I have sat up in our cold and lonely room, that used to be so brightened by her. You don't know what a trial it is, to turn aside the questions of a babbling child; to see the neighbors avoid me as I come along home, and my mates in the shop look askant at me. Oh! if it had not been that I had hard work and my little one, I should have taken to drink, or gone for a soldier! But for the child, it would have been hard not to to think (*hoarsely*) of making away with myself some way.

MIL. And leave Mary still more alone?

WAR. Poor girl! poor girl! what must be her life in there? It's a long time to look forward to until I can see her.

MIL. Why do you wait?

WAR. What! (*sternly*) when she has brought disgrace on my name, and cast a cloud on her innocent child's future. If she is suffering, so am I in sorrow, even beyond hers, for in her was set my pride, my love, my joy.

MIL. What she has done, she did for you, remember.

WAR. So it was, poor lass! (*relenting*.)

MIL. So you will go to cheer her up a little? won't you, now?

WAR. Go and see her in that dark dress, behind the railing which I put up with these hands. (*hides his eyes as if to shut out the imagined sight*) With the ring out of my voice and the peace out of my breast!

MIL. Let me not go alone, and answer her again that you would not come!

WAR. (*rises*). You are right, Milly! I will go and see her!

MIL. I knew you would when you once thought of what she suffers for you.

WAR. Yes, she was so good that the black work could have been done only for me. The shame was brought upon her, all for me, I know. I will go! I will try not to look harshly on her—only to look at her as she that I loved so dearly that the thought of separation was my greatest grief! And how are we parted now? I wont upbraid her. I will speak to her words of hope, and comfort, and consolation.

MIL. I will go with you, George. (*simply*) I know the way from having been the road so often.

WAR. *,takes her hand).* Heaven bless you, for all your kindness to my poor Mary! I will go home—home (*very pathetically*) to see baby is well—she will ask the last news of her—and then I will go. Wait till I come back.

MIL. ⌐That's a brave George! I knew you would act like this. (*exit* WARNER, L.) Oh! that's done. (*sings and waltzes about*) "A-walking in the Zoo, a-walking in the Zoo!" He will go and gladden her heart! I am so happy—I never was so happy in my life. (*changed tone*) No! I am not happy! I am miserable, very miserable, and all along of that wretch Bob Levitt! (*knock* L.) Come in! (*seated* R , *sewing*) Come in! I believe the people are all deaf in the house.

Enter, L., BOB LEVITT, *very wretched in looks and tone of voice.*

LEV. What, Milly, don't you know me?

MIL. So it is *you*, is it? (*pretendedly scornful.*)

LEV. May I come in, Milly? (*entering timidly.*)

MIL. You look as if you had come in, already. (*rises*) You are a pretty object, you are!

LEV. Then there's a couple of us, Milly. (*approaching her*) You are prettier than ever, Milly !

MIL. How dare you come to me after staying away so long while you had plenty of money ?

LEV. Don't you repulse me, Milly? The money's gone and the false friends went along with it—I haven't a valuable article to show in exchange for it. I haven t a kind face to turn to, but yours.

MIL. You had far better take yourself off. I am very angry with you, Bob Levitt.

LEV. (*dolefully).* Not half so angry as I am with myself.

MIL. You are a wretch !

LEV. Desp'rate ! or I'd never more have shown my face here.

MIL You have been on the tramp——

LEV. Till I haven't a shoe to my foot.

MIL. You have been "on the fuddle. '

LEV. Till there's not a vein in my body but jumps and throbs like a punching-machine. I've been ill treated by them that courted me in my brighter days, and I've b en kicked out of the very doors where I spent my money. No one will have me, no one will look at me, and so (*mournfully*) I have come back to you !

MIL. Like a bad shilling. Thank you, I am very proud of the preference.

LEV. I know you think badly of me. But every one has some good in him that must show some day. You don't know how ripe for repentance a man is when he is so awfully hungry and dry as me this moment. I am confoundedly ashamed of myself, and if you could make me more ashamed, I would feel obliged to you.

MIL. Oh, you *say* so.

LEV. Milly, you might make me another man. I have been bandied about till I'm dizzy and dazed. Remorse has thrown me to liquor, and liquor has thrown me back to remorse. Milly, I'm regularly going to the bad.

MIL. Regularly gone, I think.

LEV. Not yet, Milly; not yet. I have one chance yet. (*dolefully*) Milly, marry me!

MIL. Oh! (*recedes from him a little*) And go to the bad along with you. (*tosses her head*) Thank you!

LEV. Oh Milly, you can help me back to the right road. I think I could go steady in double harness, with a good clear head like yours to guide me, and your light hand on the reins. All I want is some one to love and live for. I love you, Milly. Don't say you won't have me. If you will only see some good in me, it will be there for you to bring it out.

MIL. I never heard of such a thing! such impudence! To be sure, you are very low down in the world, and I can't help but feel for you.

LEV. You don't know how welcome your pity is. You can save me from destruction here, and the devil and the deep, deep sea hereafter! (*pathetically*) Oh Milly, if ever a woman earned heaven by saving a man from the other place, you may be that woman! Dare you trust me?

MIL. You look as if you were miserable.

LEV. Not more than I feel.

MIL. Are you not ashamed of yourself?

LEV. (*groans*). Awfully!

MIL. An object of charity.

LEV. I haven't a copper.

MIL. If I forgive you, will you promise to give up drinking, and stick to your work for the next three months?

LEV. I will——

MIL. Ah, ah!

LEV. That is, I will try; and with your help—And you will have me?

MIL. (*turns away*). I will think about it.

LEV. Ah! (*joyfully.*)

MIL. Stop a bit! I have not finished with you yet. I can go on scolding you as we go over to George Warner's.

LEV. (*taken by surprise and horror*). George Warner? (*stammering, receding to* R.) I can't stand seeing him, poor fellow!

MIL. (c.). Ah! that's just like you men! You won't speak to your old mate because he is in trouble. He's not been once to see his poor wife, because she is in prison. If he had been in, she would have been there ten times a month.

LEV. How does poor Mary bear it?

MIL. Like a woman; that is, a great deal better than any man.

LEV. But she confessed that she took the box.

MIL. Who would have believed it if she had not?

LEV. Milly, she no more took it than I—(*quickly*) you!

MIL. How do you know?

LEV. (*stammering*). Why, look at her character!

MIL. Her character! You mean, then, that it must have been George. It lies between her and him.

LEV. I don't believe it was more her than George. It was—that is— I mean—

MIL. What do you mean?

LEV. Lord help me! I don't know what I mean! (MILLY *gets hat and mantle on and goes* L.) Don't mind me. It's the *D. T.* (*delirium tremens*) Don't leave me, Milly, don't leave me alone! I want drink——

MIL (*takes his hand*). You want pnysic. You are very ill, Bob Levitt, and I won't leave you till you have seen the doctor.

LEV. No, no! a drop of brandy. (*hoarsely.*)

MIL. (*firmly*). Not one! take one, and you have spoken your last word to Milly Rigg. (*drags him off* L.)

LEV. A drop of brandy! [*Exit*, L., *struggling with* MILLY.

Scene changes to

SCENE II.—*Interior of Prison in 4th grooves. Singing of hymn by Female Voices heard off stage*, R.

Enter, R. U. E., *to opening* C., TUNKS *and* WARNER.

TUNKS. Uncommon fond of singing they are, to be sure. Poor things! This is where you stand; she will come through that door (*points to* R. D.) and will stand there. There's the matron's place. But, I forgot, you have done work in this cell?

WAR. Yes. (*sadly*) I put up those rails.

TUNKS. Then you understand. There goes the lock. They are coming.

WAR. Then we will not be alone.

TUNKS. Only the matron. There's the rules and regulations. You will have twenty minutes—good measure for her sake. (*pause*) Speak kindly to her! she wants it, poor thing! and she deserves it!

[*Exit*, R. U. E.

Enter, R. D., MRS. WARNER *and* MATRON. MATRON *enters the enclosed space, and takes seat there*, R. MRS. WARNER *comes to* R. C.

MRS. W. George, my husband! (*they look at each other. Both are subdued in voice and manner up to the close of the Act, when* MRS. WARNER *gives way to her emotion in the wildest manner*) You are there, George?

WAR. Yes, Mary, I am here.

MRS. W. You are not much changed; you are paler.

WAR. That's better than I could expect.

MRS. W. It's six months since I wrote to you, and you did not answer; not even have you written to me. I don't want to reproach you, George, now that I do have you here Speak to me, George.

WAR. (*tearfully*). My poor lass, my poor lass!

MRS W. Don't cry, dear. Remember, we have only twenty minute —don't let us waste them. Dear baby, is she well and happy?

WAR. Well and happy.

MRS. W. Who have you had to take care of her?

WAR. Mrs. Russell has been very good to her, and Milly Rigg looks in often.

MRS. W. Heaven reward them. Milly has a good heart. How are you getting on?

WAR. I have not been out of work. I am at Wheeler's, with a better berth than I had at Dutton's, and ten shillings rise.

MRS. W. I am so glad of it, I am so glad of that. Does baby ask where is her mother?

WAR. Often, and that's what cuts my heart.

MRS. W. And what do you tell her?

WAR. That mother has gone away, a long way off.

MRS. W. Yes, a long way from her—(*quickly*) but you tell her that I shall come back soon. I don't mind it so very much, though five years seems so long. But they will take off a year and more of it, and (*turns *to* MATRON) I have no reports against me, do I, ma'am? (*the* MATRON *pretends to be dozing with her eyes half closed*) She don't hear us. She is a good kind soul, and we may speak out before her. I shall bear it all, George, all the sorrow and the shame. I don't mean to blame you, dear.

WAR. (*looks up surprised*). You blame me?

MRS. W. How could I prevent doing as I did?

WAR. Was the temptation so strong upon you?

MRS. W. The temptation? (*surprised—sadly*) ᵛ don't repent what I have done.

WAR. (*shocked and surprised*). You don't repent what you have done?

MRS. W. It was to save you.

WAR. To save me! Better that you had let me go down to ruin than be saved by that! (*his tone and manner, like hers, become more and more animated from this out.*)

MRS W. Oh! I don't deserve this! (*bitterly.*)

WAR. Well, what can I say?

MRS. W. I do not ask you to accuse yourself of the crime for which I suffer—no, no. I thought that you would feel for me, and would come to console me before this. Better you had not come at all, than to be coldly silent or to speak stern words.

WAR. You speak of your suffering and shame! Don't I know what shame and sorrow is—as I sit, under the weight of it, in the cloud of that crime in our desolate home, shutting out of my ears the cry of our child, for I hate to hear her ask the question which I must answer with a lie. If I had only lost my wife, the pain would have been greater, though the grief were less profound.

MRS. W. Oh! the hard-hearted cruelty of the man! I begged for a kind word of comfort, and was willing to suffer all the consequences of the guilt, and not by speech or sign to own it. (*to* MATRON) Look you, you are a woman and have a heart—look at this man, to whom I have given my love and life! When trial comes upon us, he shrinks from me; and when I am parted from my home and my child, he makes the separation all the harder to me!

MATRON (*rises*). Really I must now allow this. If you cannot speak more quietly, you cannot see your husband again.

MRS. W. You hear that, George?

WAR. (*sadly*). I hear it.

MRS. W. (*indignantly*). And say nothing? (*fiercely*) I can live without you henceforth! See if you can live without her who has been a good mother to your child and a wife more than true to your good name! Never come to see me again! Go home, George Warner, to the desolate fireside that you have made desolate, which will never know me again · to the helpless child that you have made motherless, who will never see me again! (*voice trembles a little but becomes firm again. Quickly*) It was you who put up these bars! You have this day set up a blacker separation between us—black as your unrelenting heart! strong and cold with the iron of your will—the barrier of an unrepentant spirit! (*lifts her arms as if to appeal to heaven against* WARNER. WARNER *bows his head, full of grief and surprise.* MATRON *is about to interfere and silence* MRS. WARNER.)

Picture.

* WARNER.	3 E.
* MATRON.	2 E.
* MRS. WARNER.	1 E.

CURTAIN.

ACT III.

SCENE I.—*Garret in 4th grooves. Stage dark. Moonlight effect.*

Discover MILLY *up* R., *sewing.*

MIL. (*plaintively*). How cold it is ; my fingers are too numb to do this coarse work. Oh, Bob, Bob ! I could forgive you for your neglect of me, but not for yours of our poor child. I don't care for myself. I married you with my eyes open, in spite of poor Mary's warning. While you are idling about, our poor babe is dying for want of the costly food which the doctors say alone will save him. Oh ! it is so hard not to be able to save the creature to whom one gave life. May I not murmur sometimes ? Oh, why are there rich people, who let sweet babes like mine die for want of what would never be missed out of their abundance. Alas ! if he lives, with a mother weaker each day from want of common necessaries, and a shiftless, vagrant father, how hard, poor child, will be his life. Yet I pray that Heaven will spare him ! (*knock,* L. D.) Come in !

Enter, L. D., MRS. WARNER.

MRS. W. I beg your pardon, ma'am. (MILLY *starts, rises and listens attentively*) I have not lived here long ; but I heard that your child was ill. I have had much experience in nursing children. (L. C.)

MIL. It is very ill, indeed. They say it will die. (R. C.)

MRS. W. I hope not. At any rate, we'll do what we can for it.

MIL. I have not had my clothes off these three nights.

MRS. W. Then you must have a rest. Lie down and have a sleep ; I'll sit up by baby.

MIL. You are very kind. (*takes up candle*) Will you come nearer the light ? (MRS. W. *comes into ray of light through window in* F.) Do I not know your voice ? Your face is familiar to me. (*abruptly*) I thought so ! You are Mary Warner !

MRS. W. Oh ! not that name, now ! (C.) Is it possible ! Milly Rigg ! what has brought you to this ?

MIL. Why did I not take your good advice ? I should never have married Bob Levitt——

MRS W. Levitt's wife ?

MIL. But you were not by—I'm afraid I allude to what is painful ?

MRS. W. No ! don't fear to hurt my feelings ! I have no feelings now ! I am past that.

MIL. Well, before your time was up, I listened again to his entreaties, and, in a weak moment of belief in my power to make him a good, industrious man, I consented to bear his name. (*wipes away tears*) He's not a bad husband when at his best. But how is it that you are living in a place like this ?

MRS. W. It is the house for such as I. I live here, and support myself with doing "slop-work." I don't want more than my mere existence.

MIL. But your husband ?

MRS. W. George ! (*coldly*) I do not live with hi

MIL. What ! won't he forgive you ?

MRS. W. For what I never did. It is for me to forgive him. I will tell you, for you will let it go no farther, Milly. And besides, you were by when I confessed my guilt. It was done to save my husband.

MIL. Then you did not steal——

Mrs. W. No! When George was accused, I saw it all! He had given way to the belief that he had been wronged, and saw in the ease of taking that cash-box the means to repay himself. Prompted by a noble impulse of love, I took the crime upon myself, and confessed in his stead, determined to bear all for him, that he might keep his place in the world, his name unblackened, and a home for our little child. But he feared still what I had saved him from. It was six months before he came to my prison. Then I had written to him, and you know, received no reply. That I could have borne. But when he came, and all my suspense would have been forgiven him, he was cold and cheerless as the walls around me, and I sought for a smile of comfort on his stern face, but in vain. I met him with a heart ready to overflow with pent-up love, but he was cold in tone and chary of speech. In his coward fear he would not own to the crime whose penalty I endured, and pretended a surprise that doubled his shame. His hardness froze my affection, and my love turned to hate and scorn. One word brought on another, and my words, begun in joy and tenderness, grew into bitter reproaches. We parted, he in anger, I indignant at so much baseness in the man to whom I had given so much, for whom I had parted with home and child and friends of my heart! Time passed, and my term came to a close. He had written to me, but I gave him no reply. Once was forever! When the day came of my release, I knew that he was at the doors waiting for me, but I gave him the slip, and ever since have eluded his inquiries. As I told him that day when we last stood face to face, parted by bars of his own creation, I would never see him again! And I will keep my word till I die!

MIL. (horrified). And your child?

MRS. W. (her voice changing to gentleness). Don't talk of her. If I were to think of her, I should go mad! Oh, often in the still hours, and through darkness, I feel her little hands pulling at my heart-strings. Ah! George loves the child and he will smooth her life for her own sake, if not in gratitude to me. Poor motherless one, I would cross the earth to take you to my arms again after so long; but I will return to my husband, never, never!

MIL. How you must have suffered.

MRS. W. More than I can tell, or others guess! Often I wished for the end! Two years have passed, and he has not found traces of me. No doubt he thinks me dead, and others too. That's all the better. But I forget your sorrows in my own. You must have suffered, too.

MIL. My story is soon told. A wife too ignorant to do the work that she is too weak to seek; a husband who spends his time among the idle and dissolute, as indolent and reckless as the most of them; and a child that has never known a comfort, save those its poor mother has to rob herself of to give it. We have parted with everything to live on until now. Where we are to look for another meal, or a rag to cover us, I cannot know.

MRS. W. I have no money myself—I paid away the last for rent here. But I have some owing me. Work has been scarce to me; it is hard to get rid of the jail mark! (takes wedding ring off) But here, on this you can get something. You know the neighborhood, and can find a pawn-broker; there may be one open.

MIL. Your ring!

MRS. W. (softly, half aside) I have kept it through all. As well now as later.

MIL. I can't take that? We will wait for better times.

MRS. W. Baby cannot wait. Take it. I shall have money soon, and I can get it back. You must not let the child perish for want of food.

Go! I will take care of baby till you come back. I will stay here and wait. (*goes to bed up* R.)

MIL. (*looks at bed.*) He has cried himself to sleep. (*puts on bonnet.*)

MRS. W. Take my shawl. (*gives shawl*) It is bitter cold.

MIL. God bless you. (*puts on shawl; hurriedly*) How good you are I shall not be long.   [*Exit,* L. D.

MRS. W. Poor Milly! to think of her having been brought to this strait. Others have griefs and sufferings as well as ourselves. (*takes seat by table,* L. *side of it*) How cold it is! her poor little one sleeps quietly—I can hardly hear it breathe. (*tenderly*) I wonder where my little girl is to-night? Asleep, I hope, in her nice warm bed, for he will see that she has everything she wants—all save what a mother's sharp sight could see she needs. My poor little Mary, far away from your mother, does the love of her who loves you so well, visit you in your innocent dreams. Oh! my darling! (*lets her head droop forward upon her arms on table*).

(*Voice of* LEVITT, *off* L.). Confound the stairs! Show us a light, Milly!

Enters, L. D., *lounges across to fireplace,* R. 1. E., *and seats himself there.*

LEV. Old Floyd stopped me on the stairs about the back rent, as usual. Pay rent, indeed, when we have to get along without brandy (*plays with poker.*)

MRS. W. (*up* C., *aside*). Poor Milly

LEV. Nobody doing nothing, and don't want nobody to help! Broo-oo! (*rubs his hands*) how cold it is, and it looks like snowing. No fire for a fellow, and I haven't the price of a quartern of gin to mend his boots, (*holds up foot*) worn out like the wearer on the tramp. (*pause*) How's the kid.

MRS. W. Very ill.

LEV. You don't say so, Milly. (*interested, turns round.*)

MRS. W. It is not Milly.

LEV. (*rises*). Not Milly!

MRS. W. She has gone out to get something for the child. (C.)

LEV. Not Milly! (*to* R. C.) Who is it then?

MRS W. Do you not know me? Have you forgotten Mary Warner?

LEV. Mary Warner! (*very excited*) Forgotten you! (*hoarsely*) I wish I could forget you! But is it you, or (*in terror*) your ghost! I've seen that often enough, Heaven knows! Are you real, or is it D. T.?

MRS. W. (*coldly*). I am the real Mary Warner. I heard your child cry and came in to spend the night with it, not knowing it was Milly's, my old friend's.

LEV. You came in to nurse my child? (*goes up to bed*) Is he so bad.

MRS. W. Perhaps dying!

LEV. Not that! (*opens curtain at the side and looks within*) Have I brought you to this, poor little beggar! and beggar's brat! Right you are, Bob! not a penny to put life into his little weakly body, or to get his poor father a drop of brandy to warm him this miserable weather. (*to* C., MRS WARNER *coming down and to* R. C. *front*) Where, do you say, has Milly gone?

MRS. W. Gone to the pawnbroker's.

LEV. (*surprised*). To the pawnbroker's! Well, I'm glad *she* has got something to pop! I haven't—my venerable uncle would turn up his nose at my rags.

MRS. W. (*quietly*). I lent her my wedding-ring.

LEV. So *you* have been standing my wife's friend! You find money for *my* poor child, you that got five years' penal for the robbery of that cash-box!

MRS. W. Ah! I have told the truth to you wif —I am innocent. I never took it.

LEV. Ah! (*sadly*) who knows that better than I?

MRS. W. I did not do it, though I confessed to the act.

LEV. That's what floors me. (*very excitedly*) You wait here till I come back! Don't be afraid! It's not D. T. this time—I am not going to make a hole in the water. I must find Milly! (*moves about frantically*) I'll make a clean breast of it. As well first as last—there had to be an end of it some day—I'm tired of it! What if they do give me "penal!" Milly will get along much better without me, than with such a millstone round her innocent neck. And the kid! (*staggers to bed*) No! I can't give myself up! I should feel I was making him a poor little orphan—robbing him of a father at the very time when he wants him most. I must see Milly! (*gets L.*) You wait here!   [*Exit, L. D.*

MRS. W. (*to* C). What does he mean? Is he drunk? what's that he says about knowing my innocence better than me, and making a clean breast of it? of what? Oh! if George—if George after all should not be the one—and all these years of sorrow to us both! Oh! I must see him again, and make him tell me all. (*goes L.*)

Enter, L. D., nervously, MILLY.

MIL. Oh! (*starts back, and then goes to table and looks at purse in her hand.*)

MRS. W. Have you not seen your husband?

MIL. (*hoarsely*). No! has he been in?

MRS. W. He has just gone out to meet you.

MIL. I must have passed him on the stairs. (*gives* MRS. WARNER *ring*) Never mind—I couldn't face him now. (*wipes forehead with sleeve. Gives shawl to* MRS. WARNER, *who mechanically puts it on.*)

MRS. W. What! (*sadly*) wouldn't they lend you anything on it? (*puts on ring.*)

MIL. I didn't ask. (*takes coin, leaves purse on table*) They are all closed. I met a kind gentleman in the street, and he let me have a lot of money. There's some for you.

MRS. W. How your hand trembles! how your heart beats!

MIL. (*stammers*). I have been running. (*gets basket up L. and goes to L. D.*) I will soon come back. (*aside, at L. D.*) Ah, my darling, you shan't starve now!   [*Exit, L. D., with basket.*

MRS. W. My ring has brought good luck to her. Milly, the proud and light-hearted, forced to beg! How wild she looked. (*goes to table*) She will have all she wants for the child. (*starts, takes up purse*) Four sovereigns! what a lot of money. (*starts with great surprise*) This purse! how strange! it is the very color and make of one I netted for George! the first present I made him after our marriage. Oh, then we were so happy that no one could have dreamt of such days as these. Is the night as dark to him as to me. Oh, that I might see him again! any way, any where, have the sight of my husband. (C.)

Voices, L., and scuffle. MRS. FLOYD, *entering, L.*

I tell you that it's a mistake! it can't in reason be here!

Enter, L. D., TOLLITT, TWO POLICEMEN, *several* WOMEN *and* CHILDREN *for crowd*. MRS. WARNER *goes up* C. MRS. FLOYD, R.*

MRS. W. Hush!

TOL. (C. *front*). Of course! this is the most respectable room in the most respectable house in Plumtree Court, which is the most respectable court in Westminster. Ah! (*sees* MRS. WARNER) That's you, young woman! I want you to come with us.

MRS. W. Wanted to come with you? where?

TOL. In the first place to the Rochester Road station-house.

MRS. W. Station-house?

TOL. Yes! .

MRS. W. What for?

TOL. For robbery from the person as we call it, but I suppose you would call it a lark!

POLICE. Ha, ha, ha!

MRS. W. (*aside, glancing at* MILLY, *who hangs her head*). I understand it all now! (*aloud*) Robbery! Why, I have not been out of the house this night!

MRS. FLOYD. Not she!

TOL. Of course, not!

POLICE. Ha, ha!

MRS. FLOYD (*to* TOLLIT). It's my new first-floor front lodger, and a most respectable! she pays her rent in advance!

TOL. If she didn't go out of the house this night, perhaps this puss (*takes up purse from table*) blew in at the window! (*crowd begin to murmur*) Young woman, let me give you a bit of advice, seeing as you are a new hand, the next time you go on the snatching lay, don't wear a shawl (*touches fringe of* MRS. WARNER'S *shawl*) which *babbies* might swear to, let alone Bobbies—Eh? (*to* POLICE, *who laugh*) Will you walk or ride? I should advise you to walk, as the night is chilly and I haven't got a foot warmer!

POLICE. Ha, ha!

MRS. W. (*calmly*). I will go with you. (*aside*) This time, my innocence must be proved! (*to* MRS. FLOYD) I am very sorry that this should have occurred in your house, but it is not my fault. Please tell Mrs. Levitt what I am charged with. (*aside, going* L. *with* TOLLIT) Poor Milly! I see it all now'

All form picture.

CROWD.
* * * * *

MRS. FLOYD.   TOLLIT.   MRS. WARNER.   POLICE.
             *   *   *   *

Scene closes in.

SCENE II.—*Room in Court-house in 1st grooves.*

Enter, L., SCRIVEN *and* WARNER.

SCRIVEN. I sent for you, Warner, because I have got good news for you. They've caught the woman who robbed you.

---

* MRS. WARNER.   POLICE.

MRS. FLOYD.   * TOLLIT.

C.

WAR. It is bad news; I was hoping that I should never hear anything more of it after I made the complaint.

SCRIV. Why, it seems a most flagrant case.

WAR. Who knows what tempted her ? (*sadly*.)

SCRIV. Who knows what tempted her ? The money you so imprudently displayed, of course. You are met in the street by a young woman who recites to you the usual story of poverty and misfortune. It's the common thing !

WAR. Because it is so commonly the fact.

SCRIV. Ha, ha ! I wonder that you have retained such a soft place in your heart after having been so many years abroad among the wild natives and coarse navvies.

WAR. It's the chafing of rough life that makes onet ender. True, I have been long away, and have been busy with speculations and contracts, in which I made my fortune, but I have never forgotten my early experience. I was a workman, an ordinary working man once, and I have brushed shoulders with the classes which you have seen only from the magistrate's bench.

SCRIV. I beg your pardon. We magistrates of the police courts get to sound all the depths of human misery.

WAR. You see the crime and evil that festers and swelters in the heat of passion, but not the patient wretchedness which shrinks from sight and suffers and dies up some blind alley or in the nook of a dead wall, secret to the last, too proud to beg in life, too proud to groan at death. I wish I had never met that woman. Or, given away to my first impulse, to relieve her.

SCRIV. Instead of obeying sensible second thoughts, and buttoning up your pockets.

WAR. Her sudden snatching of my purse showed how much she needed it.

SCRIV. Very likely, for drink.

WAR. Well, perhaps I take too sentimental a view of these matters, Scriven. It comes from the secret in my life. You are not an old friend, Scriven, but you are a good and true one, and I must not fear to tell you anything. I have had a sad blow in my life.

SCRIV. Yes, to be left alone with a motherless child is hard. I know what that is. We men do not know the full worth of women till we lose them.

WAR. I wish I could withdraw the charge.

SCRIV. Impossible, my dear fellow. You must not let weakness of feelings stay your duty to the public.

WAR. But can I not avoid appearing to tender my evidence ?

SCRIV. Well, that may be managed. Usher ! (*calls off*, R.)

Enter USHER, R.

Is the inspector who took that woman, charged with robbery from the person, into custody, in the court ?

USHER. Mr. Tollit ? Yes, sir.

SCRIV. Let me see him directly.   [*Exit* USHER, R.

WAR. Do you not trust the police too much ? Are they not apt to round off their stories so as to always convict.

SCRIV. Mere professional pride, that's all.

Enter TOLLIT, R., *he salutes.*

You took that woman in charge, I believe, last night ? (WARNER L., *thoughtful.*)

Tol. I did, sir.

Scriv. Do you think your evidence will suffice to convict without call-ing on this gentleman ?

Tol. I hope so, sir.

Scriv. That will do. Just tell my clerk to call you first. (*exit* Tol-lit, r.) Come, * rner ! [*Exit with* Warner, r.

Scene changes to

SCENE III.—*Interior of Court-room in 3rd grooves.*

Discover Clerk, Reporters, Police, Usher, Crowd, l. u. e. *corner.*

Enter, d. f. Levitt, Milly *and* Mrs. Floyd.

Lev. Make way there for gentlemen of the press ! (*business with* Policemen.)

Usher. Silence ! silence ! His worship the magistrate.

Enter, r. *to seats* r., Scriven *and* Warner.

Scriv. (*to* Warner, *seated*). Your case is the first one. It will be hardly necessary for you to appear—it is clear. (*aloud*) Bring in the prisoner. Robbery from the person, accused refuses to give her name.

Enter, l., Tollit *and* Two Policemen *with* Mrs. Warner. Tollit *goes up* l. c., Mrs. Warner *gets into dock* l. *front, and keeps her hands over her face.*

War. (*to* Scriven). She is ashamed, poor thing !

Scriv. No ! the usual dodge—it prevents wardens and police recog-nizing them.

Policeman (*to* Levitt, *trying to touch* Mrs. Warner). You keep back there !

Lev. Keep your own back !

Usher. Silence !

Lev. (*to* Mrs. Warner). It's all right, Mary ! we are here ! It's me and Milly ! keep your spirits up !

Mrs. W. (*looks round*). Milly here !

Lev. Don't be afraid ! speak the truth—the whole truth and nothing but the truth !

Scriv. (*to* Warner, *aside*). Did you ever see a charge-sheet ? Curious, eh ?

Mrs. W. (*glances across to* r., *aside, surprised and horrified*). George Warner ! Heaven help me ! (*staggers.*)

Mil. (*to* Policeman). Do let me to her !

Police. Keep back, young woman !

Lev. Young woman yourself ! Let the lady alone !

Usher. Silence !

Scriv. (*to* Warner). Is that the woman you gave into charge ?

War. I can't make her face out, but that is the shawl she wore.

Scriv. We will begin by taking Sergeant Tollit's evidence

Usher. Sergeant Tollit.

Tol. (*gets into witness stand up* c., *and is sworn by book*). William Tol-lit, sergeant, C. Division. (*returns book to* Clerk) I was on duty in the Rochester Road last night——

Scriv. Where ?

Tol. Westminster, sir, where I saw the party on the bench.

Scriv. Oh! the prisoner sitting in the dock?

Tol. Not the person in the dock, sir, but the gentleman on the bench.

Scriv. (*to* Warner). Oh! you are "the party on the bench." (*he and* Warner *smile.*)

Tol. And I saw the prisoner accosting him.

Scriv. What?

Tol. (*emphatically*). Accosting him, your worship.

Scriv. What do you mean by accosting him?

Tol. As females generally do accost!

Scriv. How?

Tol. She went up to the gentleman and asked him for something.

Scriv. She begged of him?

Tol. Yes, your worship.

Scriv. Well, did he give her anything?

Tol. No, your worship, but I saw him thinking of it.

Scriv. You saw the gentleman *thinking!* (*to* Warner) A new discovery in optics, eh, Warner?

Tol. He put his hand in his pocket to give her money, but then he thought better of it, and didn't give anything.

Scriv. Oh, I see.

Tol. Then she turned away as if desperate, and began to cry, which was complained of by the corner publican as disorderly conduct.

Scriv. But she is charged with robbery from the person.

Tol Which I said so, your worship. When the gentleman raised the cry, she dropped it——

Scriv. The purse?

Tol. No, she hooked it—ran away——

Scriv. Oh!

Tol. But I followed her and saw her run up into Plumtree Court——

Scriv. A bad neighborhood, I believe?

Tol. Which it is in the police books so.

Mrs. Floyd (*very loudly and fiercely*). Which it is a lie, as I have had my house there these twenty years, and never had my water cut off but twice, and that was because of the rates-collector not coming round regular, but asking wrong at number seventeen instid of number seving, which is my number!

Scriv. Ah! I suppose that's the landlady?

Tol. It is, your worship.

Scriv. Put that woman out! (Police *remove* Mrs. Floyd, d. f. Scriven *to* Warner) These landladies are generally of this description —loud voiced and tenacious of reputation. Go on. (*to* Tollit.)

Tol I sent "C. 30" round to the other end of the court, so that she couldn't pass through that way. The snow was on the ground, and I never lost sight of her, and she went into number seven. I saw a light up at the attic window. I went up stairs, and found her, with the purse and money (*points to* Clerk's *desk*) produced, in that room.

Scriv. Oh! and you recognized her?

Tol. Well, sir, it was night, and I can't say as to her face, but (*firmly*) I can swear to her shawl.

Scriv. Don't you know that it is common among women of her station to have that pattern of shawl?

Lev. (*delighted*). Hear! hear!

Usher. Silence! (*business of* Levitt *with* Police, l. u. *corner.*)

Mil. Oh, dear! (*very much distressed.*)

Scriv. You can stand down. (Tollit *leaves stand and comes around to front of railing up* c.) Warner.

WAR. (*rises, presses book which* CLERK *presents him*). George Warner. I was going along the Rochester Road, when a woman spoke to me.

SCRIV. The prisoner in the bar?

WAR. She hung her head so that I could not see her face, as if ashamed.

LEV. (*holding* MILLY *in his arms, she half fainting*). So she was.

USHER. Silence!

WAR. I can only swear that she wore a shawl like that worn there. She told me a sad story——

SCRIV. Of course! Well, is this the purse that she snatched from your hands?

WAR. Yes; it is one without a second, and very dear to me as a keepsake.

MRS. W. (*sobs*). Oh!

WAR. Some of the contents are gone, and, of course, I cannot swear to the loose coin. It contained about six pounds.

SCRIV. (*to* MRS. WARNER). Take your hands down, how can the gentleman see if he can recognize you if you hide your face.

WAR. Never mind, I have already said that I would not know her by her face. (*resumes his seat.*)

SCRIV. Prisoner, you have heard the evidence, what have you to say to the charge?

MRS. W. (*keeping her hands to her face*). I say that I am innocent. I was not out of the house all that night.

SCRIV. An alibi. Have you any witnesses in support.

MRS. W. No.

LEV. Yes! Me and my wife—worse luck! (*drags* MILLY *around railing to* C., *up. Business with* TOLLIT, *who is resisted by* LEVITT *defiantly.*)

SCRIV. (*whispers with* CLERK). Mr. Tollit, do you say that you think, with a remand, you could bring proof of the prisoner's former conviction as a thief?

MRS. W. (*violently holding out her hands*). Are these the hands of a thief? (*she meets* WARNER'S *eyes. Start of both in full recognition*) Oh! (*hides her face again and turns her head* L.)

SCRIV. Sergeant, look at her hands. You are more skilled at that kind of reading than I. (TOLLIT *takes* MRS. WARNER'S *hands*) What do they say?

TOL. Left fore-finger much torn as by the needle, and both palms hardened as by charing

SCRIV. Eh! that's not like a thief's!

WAR. (*rising*). That is not the woman who took my purse!

SCRIV. Not the woman! Why you said that you could not recognize her by her face?

WAR. Yes, but I know her voice. That is not it—I swear that is not woman.

SCRIV. Then she need not call witnesses in her defence. Prisoner is discharged. Call the next case.

LEV. A jolly good job for us! (MRS. WARNER *leaves dock hastily.*)

WAR. Stop that woman—I want to speak to her

TOL. (*pushes* POLICE *aside*). No!

MRS. W. Let me go! I want to go! (*goes to* L. D.)

TOL. (*to* POLICE). You have no right to stop her. She is discharged.

WAR. (*frantically*). I must speak to her.

ALL *form picture.*

TOLLIT *keeps* POLICE *from touching* MRS. WARNER *going to* L. D. WARNER
  is detained by SCRIVEN. ALL *are on their feet, excited.*

  * SCRIVEN.   * LEVITT.   * MILLY.   POLICE.
                                                           *   *
              * CLERK.
  * WARNER.   * TOLLIT.   * MRS. WARNER.

                    CURTAIN.

                    ACT IV.

SCENE I.—*Street in 6th grooves. Gas down. Moonlight,* L. 1 E., *ready to
  fall on* R. *front. Gas ready turned on to light in lamps up* R. *set.
  Snow falls at intervals. Music, mournful.*

  Enter, slowly, as if tired, MRS. WARNER, L. U. E., *to* R. *front.*

MRS. W. There's no one following me. I have given them all the slip.
(R. *front*) I am at home at last. (*bitterly*) At home. This is my *home!*—
To think that I should have seen him sitting on the bench beside the
magistrate, well dressed and with all the looks of what they call a gentleman—while I am what he gave me in charge as—a prisoner in the
dock! I never knew till then the depth of sorrow and shame. (*feels in
her pockets*) At least, he cannot think me the thief. I have not got the
key, and must ring up Mrs. Floyd. (*pulls bell-pull. Bell rings* R.) He
must not find me here. But that is not likely, for he does not know
these places as I do. Some one is coming at last. (*on doorstep,* L. *end of it*)
I am wearied and eager for even my poor bed.

  MRS. FLOYD *opens* R. 1. E. D., *and stands in door-way.*

MRS. F. Pretty hours these, ma'am! (*very angrily.*)
MRS. W. I beg your pardon, I am very sorry to have disturbed you.
MRS. F. (*sharply*). And very sorry you should be! I can't have par-
ties in my respectable house who take other parties' purses to other
parties' rooms.
MRS. W. But it was a mistake, I was discharged.
MRS. F. Which I knows, as I was in the court myself, till I was put
out by the nasty obnoxious perlice—I dare say they have got me down
in their books now, me! Mrs. Jemmia Floyd, of Number 7 Plumtree
Court.
MRS. W. It is so late to-night that I can't find a room. I am very
tired. Let me in, and I will go away to-morrow.
MRS. F. To-morrow won't do for me. Out you are and out you keep.
Them's my sentiments, and what I says, I sticks to! You can send for
your box to-morrow. My first-floor back has given notice, and I expect
the rest will foller if I encourages such goin's on. That's all. Good
night, you can steal off. (*slams door.*)
MRS. W. (*alone*). Ah! (*snow falls*) That man would follow me and
persecute me after all I have given up for his sake—to enable him to
hold up his head among the proud and wealthy. The last sacrifice is

made now. I am still being punished for his crime. He has gone back
to his luxurious home, while I am thrust without a shelter, in these
rags, into the snow. My little Mary will never know how her mother
died. They say that to them who are overtaken by the frost and the
snow-falls, death comes like a sweet and peaceful sleep. (*sits on door
step*) Come so to me, kind death. (*lies down on door step*) Come to me
—for I am weary—weary of this life (*sleeps. Moon on R. 1. E.*)

*Enter, R. U. E., whistling, a lamplighter who lights lamps R. and exits, R. U.
E., whistling until he is well off. Pause. Enter R. U. E., TUNKS, well
wrapped up.*

TUNKS. Plumtree Court? Here we are! Five—six—seven. That's all
right. (*comes to R. 1. E.*) I wonder if they're awake. Hullo, here's a
young woman drunk on the door step, or she would not take the stone for
a bed such a night as this. I say, wake up! (*touches MRS. WARNER*)
Get up, I want to get to the door.
MRS. W. (*faintly*). Let me sleep!
TUNKS. I want to go in. Wake up! (*shakes her*) You will get your
death of cold. (*recognizes her on turning her face to the light*) What!
Mary Warner! What are you doing here? (*helps her to her feet, she re-
mains weak and trembling.*)
MRS. W. Waiting for death. Oh, let me die!
TUNKS. Not if James Tunks, prison warder, and as such, one of the
authorities, knows it! Rouse up! I am your old friend Tunks! Don't
you remember me at Brixton? What's brought you here?
MRS. W. The landlady will not let me in.
TUNKS. By what right? Oh! I see—you are behind hand with your
rent?
MRS. W. No, it is not that. But I was arrested last night for robbery.
TUNKS. Oh, robbery! (*aside*) Poor thing! once to the well, always to
it till they get broken!
MRS. W. But I was innocent. Oh! say that you, who have known
me so long, believe me innocent!
TUNKS. I do believe you, my girl.
MRS. W. Thank Heaven there is somebody believes me, yet.
TUNKS (*half aside*). Her landlady turns her out of doors, she is cast
into prison, she lies down broken-hearted to die—it is hard lines on her
very hard lines. Look here! (*struts up to bell-pull and pulls it hard,*
That shows that James Tunks means business. (*to MRS. WARNER*) I came
here to see Mrs. Levitt, Milly Rigg that was, but I am glad that I
dropped atop of you, that I am, Mary.
MRS F. (*opens R. 1 E. D*). Now then! (*very sharply*) do you think
doorbells is barrel-h'organs! Oh! (*sees MRS. WARNER*) it's you at your
games again? (*to TUNKS*) So you've took her up again?
TUNKS. I'll take you down, you horrid old flint! how dare you shut
out a lodger who has paid all her rent!
MRS. F. (*stammers*). But she's been in the courts——
TUNKS. How would you look in the courts if she had been found in
the morning on your door-step, you d—d old catamaran!
MRS. F. Cata'maryann!
TUNKS. I'll let you know what it is! I am James Tunks, one of her
Majesty's authorities. This is a good young woman, and I am fond
and proud of her. Show me the way to Mrs. Levitt's rooms! look sharp
and no grumbling, or it won't be pleasant to stand in your shoes! (*draws
MRS. WARNER with him through R. D., and MRS. FLOYD humbly shuts the
door.*)

Scene closes in.

SCENE II.—*Room in 1st cut of 1st grooves.   Gas down three-quarter turn.*

Enter, R , TUNKS, MRS. WARNER *and* MRS. FLOYD.   TUNKS *to* L.   MRS. WARNER C., *and* MRS. FLOYD R.

TUNKS. Come along, Mary my dear.   Have you any such thing as a chair here ? (*gets chair* L. E. *and places it* L. C. *for* MRS. WARNER)   Sit down, my dear. (MRS. W. *takes seat.*)

MRS. F. This is Mrs. Levitt's room.   She is not home, but she won't be long. (*goes to curtains,* L. C.)   Here is her baby—sleeping as quiet as a h'oyster, like a pretty darling that it is.

TUNKS. A nice article you are to talk of pretty little darlings and babbies—you that shut your doors on honest, *hard* working women.

MRS. F. But think of my character !

TUNKS. (*mocking her tone*). " Your character ! " A pretty character you would have got from the magistrate if she had been frozen to death on your step.

MRS F. But the name of the 'ouse.

TUNKS. A nice name your 'ouse would get with a coroner's inquest on the step.

MRS. W. I wish I had !

TUNKS (*goes to her*). No, Mary, you don't wish anything half so wicked as that. (*to* MRS. FLOYD) Have you got such things as pen and ink about the place ?

MRS. F. Rayther! there's a beautiful *chany* inkstand that I won at the shilling-go at the Christian Palace.

TUNKS. Well, as Mrs. Levitt is not here, I will write her a note to explain her not finding you (*meaning* MRS. WARNER) when she comes back. [*Exit* MRS. FLOYD, R.

MRS. W. Am I going away ?

TUNKS. I should rayther think so ! The right way. You shall go home with me to my house in Brixton Avenue. One of my daughters has left home, and you can have her room, and her place at the table, my dear.

MRS. W. But I must do work ?

TUNKS. I'll find you work so that you can live like a lady.

MRS. W. And I must pay my rent ?

TUNKS. Or I'll be down upon you sharp and heavy, never you fear about that ! So get your traps ready.

Enter, R., MRS. FLOYD.

MRS. F. (*holds out pen and inkstand*). Here they are, sir.

TUNKS. So that's your shilling's worth of the *Christian* Palace, is it ? (*takes pen,* MRS. FLOYD *holding inkstand*) When you were there, I suppose you were one of the Odd Fellows ? (*writes in his memorandum-book*) Do you call this a pen ? It's more like a skewer.

MRS. F. Everybody in the 'ouse has used it and the tailor next door, and this is the first complaint I have had about it in a month.

TUNKS. Oh !

MRS. F. You must have spoilt the nib ?

TUNKS. I'll spoil your nib ! This *ink* is as thick as treacle, and full of flies.

MRS. F. They gets in there, poor things, to be out of the way of the spiders !

TUNKS. Because you charge them too much rent! (*gives note*) Give this to Mrs. Levitt when she comes in. And call a cab.

MRS. F. (*staggered with surprise*). Call a what?

TUNKS. A cab! I suppose you have seen such an animal as a Hansom now and then! And mind! if you lose that note, you will have to answer for it to the authorities—(*takes* MRS. WARNER R.)—you black-hearted. mulberry-faced old beast! [*Exit R., with* MRS. WARNER.

MRS F. (*staggers back to chair L. C., and falls into it, her arms out, pen in one hand, inkstand in the other; fans herself with pen, pants for breath, etc.*). Me a mulberry-faced beast! Oh! if only Mr. Floyd was living now, him that fell from a scaffolding in the Westminster Bridge Road and was picked up for dead in Guy's Hospital, that man would never have walked out of the house alive. To abuse me in my own room! me that slaves and starves to keep the house respectable from morning till night without a drop of consolation. (*mechanically lifts the inkbottle to her lips, but discovers her error, rises and puts pen and ink and chair off L.*) There goes the cab, as I live! Well, I never! That's the first cab I have seen in Plumtree Court as long as I have been here, except one to take Mrs. Fenn to the Fever Hospital. (C.) And how people can ride in them cabs when they don't know who has been in them last, is more than I can see. I don't object to omnibusses or even the underground railway, but no cabs for my money. (*bell, off R.*) There's some one come in. Oh! they're coming up. The back kitchen must have let them in.

Enter, R., MILLY *and* LEVITT.

There's been a gentleman here inquiring for you, ma'am. (*respectfully,* R. C.)

LEV. A gent inquiring about my wife. Hullo, what's the game. (C., MILLY L. C.)

MRS. F. Golden sovereigns is his game. (*shows coin*) He gave that to me.

LEV. For me? (MRS. FLOYD *drops her hand to evade his snatch.*)

MRS. F No, for me! There's the card he left for you, ma'am, when he couldn't see you. (*gives* MILLY *card and note.*)

LEV. See my wife. I'll see him first!

MIL. Why, this is about Mrs. Smith.

LEV. Smith? (MILLY *makes a sign to him*) Oh!

MRS. F. She's gone away!

LEV. *and* MIL. Gone away!

MRS. F. Gone away with a person in uniform who said he was one of the authorities. If he wasn't a policeman, leastwise he was next door to it—for he gave me the wust of bad language! He called me a cata-maran, and a mulberry-faced old beast! Pretty language from one of the authorities!

LEV. (*to* MILLY). What does it say?

MIL. (*reads note*). Oh! it's Mr. Tunks, the warden at Brixton, who has taken her home to his house on Brixton Avenue. How well I remember it—the pretty cottage, half-overgrown with flowers—nothing like this!

MRS. F. (*proudly*). In course not! How could you expect a cottage in the country to be like a 'ouse in town!

LEV. What's the nob with the card?

MIL Hush! (*motions that she wants* MRS. FLOYD *to be sent out.*)

LEV. (*to* MRS. FLOYD). Well, old girl, if you have finished your row, suppose you vacate our ap-par-ti-mongs.

MRS. F. Your what?

Lev. (*with French shrug of shoulders*). Our ap-par-ti-mongs!
Mrs. F. (*backing to* R. *before* Levitt, *following her up*). Ah! Mr.
Levitt, you are always at it with your chaff'!
Lev. Lor' bless you, that ain't chaff—that's French!
Mrs. F. That's much the same thing. (Levitt *will not let her pass
either side of him so that she has to go out* R.) Well! (*with affected gayety*)
It's a merry heart that never grieves! What's the odds while you are
happy!   [*Exit,* R. D.
Mil. Bob, it's George Warner!
Lev. George Warner! (*aghast*) And this is his address on the card?
(*reads card*) "8 Cromwell Place."
Mil. Where's that?
Lev. It's one of those new mushroom built squares where there used
to be open fields, and where they growed the spring rhubarb out by
Brompton way. A swell place!
Mil. He that was your mate in the workshop six years ago!
Lev. Him with four hundred pounds a year and I with four bob a
week, and behind at that.
Mil. Bob, we must bring them together! You take care of baby
while I go to George, and tell him of Mary.
Lev. (*abruptly*). Stop, Milly. I have something to tell you that has
been hanging round my neck these five years, and dragging me down,
and you and innocent kid, like the curse it is. Milly, do you remem-
ber, when the cash-box of Dutton & Downes was stolen?
Mil. Yes, yes.
Lev. Mary Warner never did it, though she confessed to it.
Mil. I know it. George Warner took the box.
Lev. Eh! who says so?
Mil. Mary told me so. Don't let it go further.
Lev. But it was not George
Mil. Not George!
Lev. It was me, Milly.
Mil. You! I will not believe it!
Lev. Yes, me! I was hid in the washing-place and heard George and
his wife talk of their want of money. When the coast was clear, I
crept out and went away with the cash-box.
Mil. And you have let Mary rest under that burden of pain and
doubt and loss of love all this time? Oh, Bob! Bob! no wonder
nothing prospered with us. There is only one course now. Bob, you
must make a clean breast of it. You go to George and tell him all,
while I go to poor Mary.
Lev. I will, Milly! I will! Oh, if I had only known that I should feel
so much better, I should have had the satisfaction of a clean breast five
years ago, though I had got five years penal for it. Can you forgive me
and give me a kiss, Milly? (*they embrace*) Oh! it's such a relief, you
can't think! I feel like another man already! Give me another! (*they
embrace*) Ah! I never was so wild with joy! But it's not D. T. this
time!   [*Exit,* R., *with* Milly.

Scenes changes to

SCENE III.—*Interior in 2d cut of 1st grooves. Gas same.*

Enter, L., Servant, *bowing in* Scriven, *in full evening dress.*

Serv. None of the company is here, sir
Scriv. (*looks at watch*). It is past seven.

Serv. But the party is put off.

Scriv. Oh !

(*Voice of* Little Mary, r.). Papa ! papa !

Serv. This is Miss Warner. [*Exit*, r.

Enter, r., Little Mary *running*

Mary. Oh ! it is not papa.

Scriv. (*takes* Mary's *hands*, c.). No, it is not your papa. It is only a friend of papa and of you, my little girl, who wishes you joy on your birthday.

Mary. Yes, everybody has wished me joy, except papa, and he does nothing but cry. Papas shouldn't cry on their little girls' birthdays, should they, now ?

Scriv. Certainly not, grown-up people should only cry on their own birthdays.

Mary (*looking* l.). Oh, here's papa !

Enter, l., Warner, who *takes* Mary's *hand*.

War. In full dress ! Then you have not been told that the party is put off?

Scriv. Yes, from your servant. What is the cause ? Has a contract to build a railway to the Mountains of the Moon failed ? (*laughingly*.)

War. No ! all is right in business matters. (*to* Mary). Mary, my darling, run and see what Miss Barker has for you. (*exit* Mary, l., *aside*) I must tell some one—it is killing me to keep it secret. (*aloud*) My friend, my kind friend, you have heard, like all my associates, that my wife was dead. Like the rest, I thought so too. But I have seen her this morning.

Scriv. Seen her—this morning ?

War. It was not she, I am sure, that I met the night of the robbery, and yet I saw her this morning in the dock at your court.

Scriv. What ! that woman !

War. Yes, listen. I was a workman in an engineering works, and had a good home, and, I thought, a blameless wife. One day she and I not together, were left in the office of my employers, and, soon after, the cash box left in an open desk, was missed. When they came to arrest me, on suspicion, she confessed that she alone had done it, knowing my eagerness to go to America, and she was sentenced to five years in prison. For a time, my hurt pride made me cold towards her, and I would not write to her or see her. At last, strongly urged, I went one day to her prison. I saw her behind the grating that I had myself put up. Heaven knows that my heart was breaking, but she saw nothing of my emotion, and reproached me as if I was the author of the crime. On one bitter reproach rushed another, and we parted, she vowing never to see me again. When her release came, which was early, thanks to her good conduct, she eluded my anxious watch, and disappeared until this time. Weary of fruitless search, I went abroad. All essays prospered with me, and I returned home rich in pocket, sad in heart. How can I meet my little girl, her child, with joy, and receive any guests to-night.

Scriv. My poor friend, I feel for you. But at least, the unhappy woman was not the principal in this last crime.

War. Not even the accomplice I believe and trust. All her manner affected me so that I have doubts which never came so strongly to me before.

SCRIV. Perhaps some explanation with her ?
WAR. Will serve to a more quiet life for me ? I hope so. I have in
quiries on foot now that may bring about our interview.

Enter, R., SERVANT.

SERVANT. A man by appointment, sir—gives the name of Levitt.
WAR. A man ! oh, he has come instead of his wife. (*to* SERVANT)
Tell him I will be in the study at once. (*Exit* SERVANT R. WARNER *to*
SCRIVEN) It is an old friend of mine, who knows my wife's present
whereabouts. It will be well, perhaps, to question him before you.
(SCRIVEN *bows. They exeunt* R.)

Scene changes to

SCENE III.—*Interior in 5th grooves. Gas up. Stage clear. Music.*

Enter, slowly, as if awe-stricken, C. D. *from* R. U. E., MILLY *and* MRS.
WARNER. MILLY *comes down* L. C., MRS. WARNER *down* C.

MRS. W. (*looking round*). Oh ! what beautiful furniture ! and all is so
bright ! No wonder that people who live in houses like these are differ-
ent from those in our court.
MIL. They are sometimes just as unhappy (*aside*) Bob is telling him
now. (*aloud*) There is kindness in hearts under these roofs, and I am
sure you will do well if you have the good wishes of the owner here.
MRS. W. How did you find out this charitable lady ?
MIL. Oh ! many of such people have persons who do nothing but go
about to find such as are worthy of their cares.

SERVANT *enters* R.

SERVANT. Master will see you now, ma'am.
MIL. I thank you.   [*Exit* SERVANT, R.
MRS. W. Master.
MIL. Oh ! it's the lady's husband. Ladies must have husbands like
other folks. I will be back soon. (*goes* R.) Don't despair, Mary ! the
clouds are breaking now, and one sunbeam is always followed by a host.
I foresee good coming.   [*Exit,* R.
MRS. W. (*alone*). Always hopeful and cheering, dear Milly ! Seeing
the light when others are under the shadow. Yet I do feel hopeful, as
if the air here was pure and sweeter than in our miserable dens. It is
so bright here ! Where is my happy home, where the sun shone ever ?
not a scrap left of the wreck. (*goes up* C. *and to* R. C. *up*) Ah ! (*sees cup
on étagère*) that cup ! it is the very image of that one ! (*sobs*) the one I
gave George ! I will ask the lady of the house for it—and perhaps
she will give it to me.

Enter, L., LITTLE MARY.

MARY. I thought papa was here. You have not seen papa, have
you ?
MRS. W. No ! I am waiting to see your mamma, dear.
MARY (*surprised*). My mamma?
MRS. W. Yes, she promised me some work.
MARY. You must be making some mistake. I have no mamma ; my
mamma died so long ago that I hardly remember I ever had one at all.

MRS. W. I beg pardon. I meant, the lady of the house.

MARY. Why, that's me! I am the lady of the house! I make papa call me the lady of the house. It's so foolish of papa to say I must wait till I am old enough. Am I not old enough! I am quite a woman grown!

MRS. W. How old are you?

MARY. I am seven years old, and this is my birthday. I am going to have my old nurse here to see me! won't that be nice?

MRS. W. (*absently*). Very nice indeed! seven years old. I wish you joy. (*tearfully*) Oh! dear me! (*takes chair R. C. R. of table front.*)

MARY. Oh! what's the matter! (*goes to her*

MRS. W. Never mind me.

MARY. What's made you cry?

MRS. W. I shall be better soon. My darling, my darling! (*sobbing.*)

MARY. But you really mustn't on my birth-day. What are you crying for?

MRS. W. I beg your pardon, miss. But I have got a little girl at home, whose birthday is to-day, and she is also seven.

MARY. Oh! (*claps her hands*) You must bring her here, and she shall see my doll and toys, and we'll be so happy!

MRS. W. Don't, my darling! (*tearfully throughout.*)

MARY. I don't like it a bit!. I hate to hear you weep! (*tries to soothe* MRS. WARNER) Don't, don't, don't, poor lady! (*pettishly*) I won't love you at all if you cry. You are as bad as papa, who has done nothing but cry to-day.

MRS. W. With joy, my darling, no doubt. It must be something most happy to be such a father. May I know his name?

MARY. Don't you know that papa is Mr. Warner. Why, everybody knows that. My name is Mary Warner.

MRS. W. Warner! Is that your name? (*very passionately*) Then you, you, you are my child! (*embraces* MARY) my child, my darling, my long lost, my angel! (*kisses her*) my own! (*looks at her*) Yes, George's eyes! (*kisses her*) and my hair! (*weeps over her*)

MARY (*struggling*). You hurt me—you must be mad!

MRS. W. (*calmer*). I am mad. (*sobbing*) Don't mind me. (*presses hand to her forehead*) I thought you were my little girl, my child! Don't call! don't tell your papa that I spoke to you. He might be angry. Don't tell your papa! for I am going away—far away, and you will never see me again. Try to think it *was* your own mamma, come back to see you and love you for a moment! Won't you give me a kiss! (*kisses* MARY) You won't mind if I cut one little piece of hair. (*takes scissors from table.*)

Enter WARNER, R. D.

One little piece—only one piece—no one will find it out

WAR. Mary!

MRS. W. George Warner! (*starts to her feet; fierce tone*) Don't touch me! (*to* C., WARNER R. C.) I have not told her! I am going away! I did not know——

WAR. But I know all! That cowardly scoundrel Bob Levitt has confessed all.

MRS. W. All—what

WAR. That he stole the cash-box from Dutton & Downes.

MRS. W. Then, it was not you! And I could think you guilty? Oh! (*falls into* WARNER'S *arms.*)

WAR And I *have* been guilty! guilty of doubting the bravest, sweetest wife man ever had! Only for that cur, we might have not had five years full of regrets.

MRS. W. Can you forgive me?

WAR. Forgive you! why, I have nothing to forgive. But let the past burn up its ashes! A bright future is now before us, and we will never look back to the black border of such a broad ocean of happiness. Come here, darling! (*takes* MARY *s hand*) This is the precious birthday present I promised you—your mother! The mother of whom you have heard me so often speak.

MARY. I know her already. She loves me very much.

MRS. W. She will love you still more as each day dawns on us. George, my husband! (*they embrace.*)

MARY. And you will never cry any more.

WAR. Never!

MRS. W. Yes, we will often! but they will be tears of joy! of sweetest happiness, that wells up from the heart without a care!

Picture. They embracing and MARY *with a hand held by each of them.*

CURTAIN.

PROPERTIES—(*See Scenery.*)

ACT I.—*Scene 1st.*—Maps, plans, cut out patterns of parts of machines; models of engines, marine, locomotive, pumpings, etc.; pair of compasses, to open, for Warner; a metal faucit for Levitt to enter with; rules, spirit level and other engineering tools, on table up L.; bankbills—coin in cash-box with bankbills; umbrellas in hat-rack, or under row of hat pegs up R. 3 E. corner; blank books on desk; paper on table up L.; stools and office arm-chairs; tool-basket for Levitt. *Scene 3d.*—Cradle, head to the audience, empty; chairs, table; apron for Mrs. Warner, L. D., without; writing materials on sideboard up C.; table-cloth, plates, etc., for three; pie in dish in oven; kettle holder, chisel on sideboard up C.; drawings on flats. ACT II.—Two chairs, table, sewing for Milly. *Scene 2d.*—Bunch of keys for Mrs. Frenwick; a framed card with head-line. Regulations stuck on R. 2 E. flat. ACT III.—*Scene 1st.*—Chairs, stools, washbasin, bed, table; candle in bottle; wedding ring for Mrs. Warner; purse and coin for Milly's second entrance; basket, clubs for two policemen. *Scene 2d.*—Rod for usher. *Scene 3d.*—Bible, writing materials on desk of magistrate and clerk. Clock on flat. ACT IV.—*Scene 1st.*—Snow and snow-cloth; spirits and sponge on end of rod for lamplighter; limelight, L. 1 E. *Scene 2d.*—Bed curtains L. on F., chair L., proscenium E.; pen and ink, note-book and card for Tunks, gold coin for Mrs. Floyd. *Scene 4th.*—Gilt cup of Act I, Scene 2d, on shelves, R. 3. E.; albums on table, limelight to show light on fountain, C. U. E.

STAGE DIRECTIONS.

R. means Right of Stage, facing the Audience; L. Left; C. Centre; R. C. Right of Centre; L. C. Left of Centre. D. F. Door in the Flat, or Scene running across the back of the Stage; C. D. F. Centre Door in the Flat; R. D. F. Right Door in the Flat; L. C. F. Left Door in the Flat; R. D. Right Door; L. D. Left Door; 1 E. First Entrance; 2 E. Second Entrance; U. E. Upper Entrance; 1, 2 or 3 G. First, Second or Third Groove.

| R. | R. C. | C. | L. C. | L. |

☞ The reader is supposed to be upon the stage facing the audience.